BIRMINGHAM CITY
FOOTBALL CLUB
- 1875 -

KEEP RIGHT ON

The Official Centenary Of St. Andrew's

Sport Media
A Trinity Mirror Business

Celebrating the official centenary of St. Andrew's, award-winning writer Hyder Jawad has collated many magical memories from the last 100 years which is sure to prove a lasting legacy in the club's history. This official book majors on the unmatchable photographic archive of the Birmingham Post & Mail, with the pictures telling the story of a century of action at St. Andrew's, reviving memories of famous matches and club heroes who feature prominently as the story of the stadium unfolds, from 1906 to 2006.

Written by:
HYDER JAWAD

Research and Design:
JAMES CLEARY

Sport Media
A Trinity Mirror Business

Executive Editor: KEN ROGERS Editor: STEVE HANRAHAN
Production Editor: PAUL DOVE Art Editor: RICK COOKE
Sales and Marketing Manager: ELIZABETH MORGAN
Designers: LEE ASHUN, GLEN HIND,
COLIN SUMPTER, BARRY PARKER, ALISON GILLILAND
Writers: ALAN JEWELL, GAVIN KIRK, DAVID RANDLES,
CHRIS McLOUGHLIN, JOHN HYNES, WILLIAM HUGHES

Published in Great Britain in 2006 by: Trinity Mirror Sport Media,
PO Box 48, Old Hall Street, Liverpool L69 3EB.

ISBN 1 9052 6616 2
978 1 9052 6616 2

Photographs: Birmingham Post & Mail. Trinity Mirror.
Additional images: ACTION IMAGES

Printed by Scotprint, Haddington, Scotland.

Contents

For centuries, it was an expanse of mud. Without a name and, seemingly, without a purpose, the field on Garrison Lane, Birmingham — "a wilderness of stagnant water and muddy slopes" — had little to commend it.

But a year before work was completed in 1906, Harold Morris visualised something special, something unique; something that would become a unique focal point for millions of Brummies.

By the time of its 50th anniversary in 1956, when Birmingham reached the FA Cup final, St Andrew's was among the most atmospheric stadiums in Britain. The experience was not always comfortable but attending a match at St Andrew's was always exhilarating. Whether in times of prosperity or depression, the supporters of Birmingham City would sing that famous hymn, 'Keep Right On', and would promote a sense of community.

The stadium has changed over the years. The terraces have been replaced by seats but the atmosphere — the humour, the savage charm — has stayed the same, turning St Andrew's into a bastion of character.

St Andrew's celebrated its 100th birthday on Boxing Day 2006. It is unlikely that it will celebrate its 200th birthday on Boxing Day 2106, but that will only serve to confirm that Birmingham will have moved on into a new era.

Birmingham have tried to vacate St Andrew's before and will do so again. That is the nature of a changing game and a changing city. There will be a Birmingham City without St Andrew's but there cannot be a St Andrew's without Birmingham City.

The expanse of mud off Garrison Lane owes everything to the club that owns it.

But in many respects, the club and the stadium are inextricably linked, just as Arsenal and Highbury are linked; just as Manchester City and Maine Road are linked. A club can move easily into the future but will always be grateful for its past. And much of Birmingham City's past — great moments or otherwise — took place at St Andrew's.

I attended my first match at St Andrew's in 1994, a Birmingham City home match against Tranmere Rovers. That was when the stadium was in transition; when David Gold was in the process of moving St Andrew's into the 21st century. I remember talking to Jasper Carrott and Joe Gallagher and coming away with a feeling of what life is like for those who have played an important part in the history of the club and, indeed, of the city.

Everybody will agree that the nadir came in May 1985 when supporters rioted during the Birmingham City-Leeds United match, turning the pitch into a war zone. The zenith of St Andrew's, however, is rather more difficult to ascertain. It is all about personal preference.

Older gentlemen will recall the glory days of the mid-Fifties, yet was there a more significant victory than when Birmingham City ripped Liverpool to pieces at St Andrew's in February 2005?

This was when it all clicked into place for Birmingham against the team who, three months later, would be crowned European champions for the fifth time. Liverpool's revenge came a year later when they defeated Birmingham, at the same stadium, by 7-0. Birmingham would soon be relegated. Their goalless draw against Newcastle United in April 2006 at St Andrew's sealed their fate.

St Andrew's can be a cold place, even in July, but its appeal has little to do with its architecture and aesthetics. Its appeal lies in those people who go there regularly and turn it into a cauldron. Even amid the tears and the pain after relegation, there were supporters who stayed behind to chant 'Birmingham, Birmingham' and sing 'Keep Right On'.

St Andrew's is a theatre. It has required much refurbishment over the years, and not all of the teams representing Birmingham there have been good, but these are peripheral issues. What matters most is that a great club has a great home so that its great supporters can fantasise about great football. Yes, St Andrew's has been a place to share dreams.

Hyder Jawad

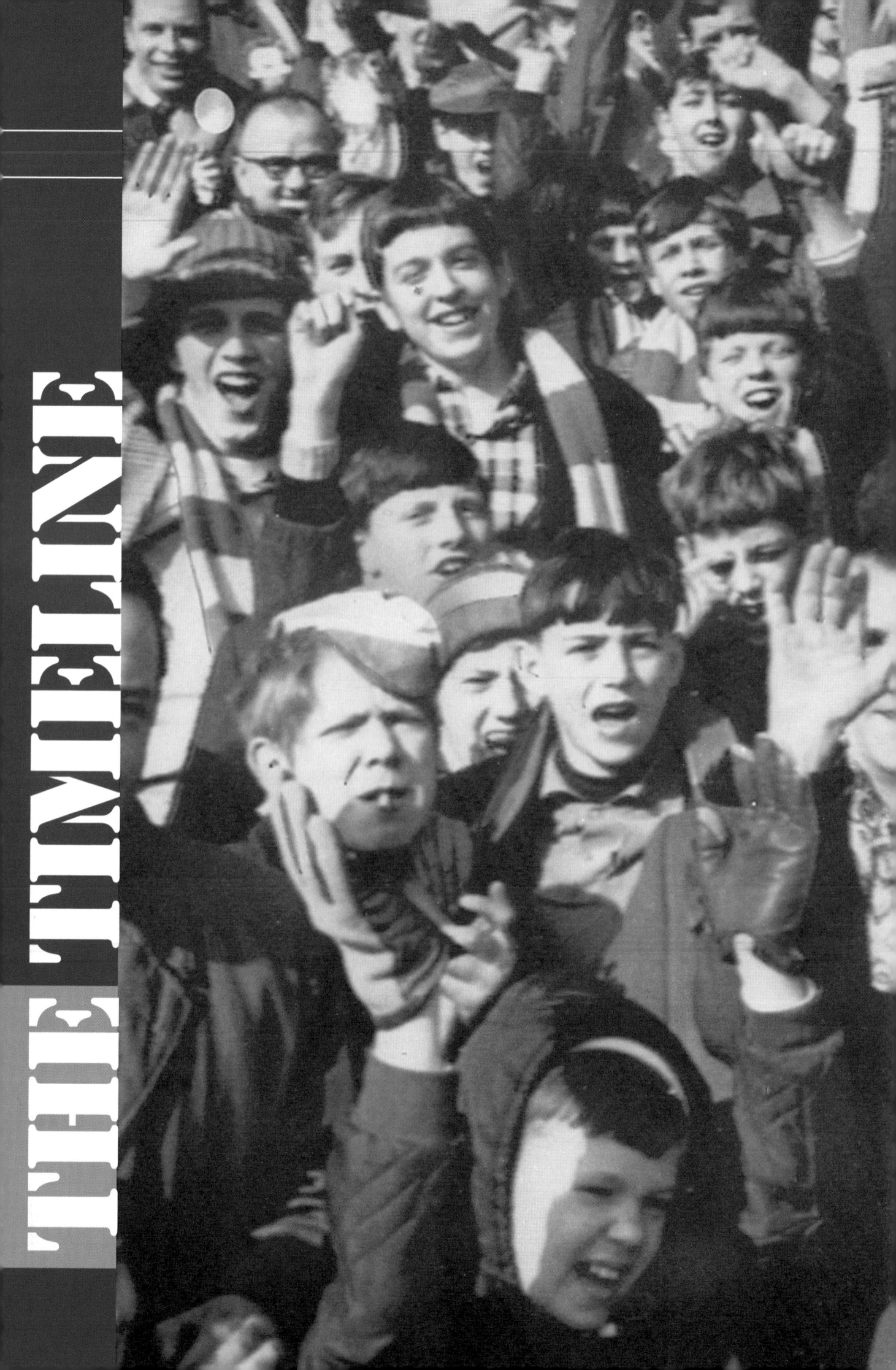

THE TIMELINE

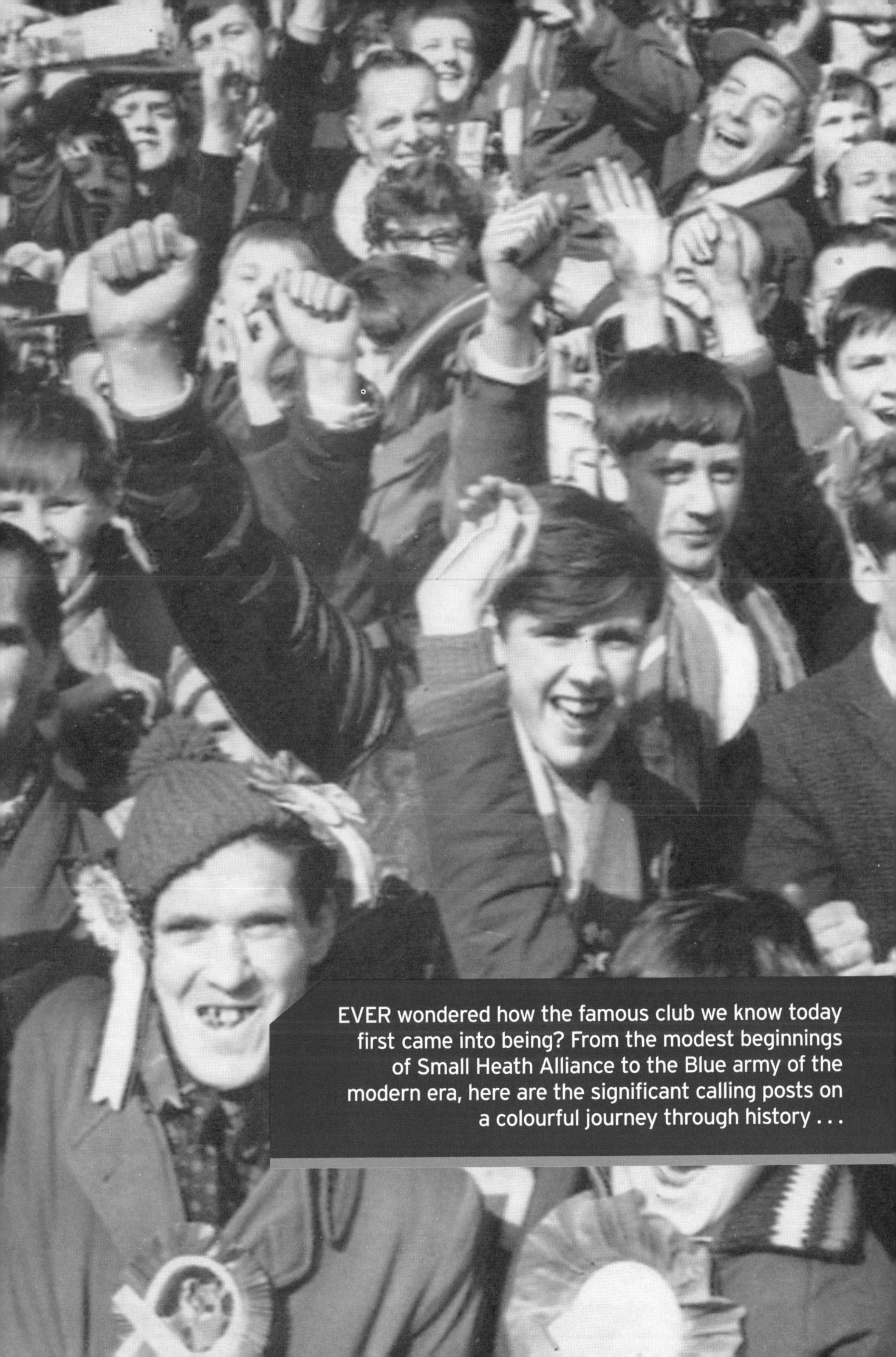

EVER wondered how the famous club we know today first came into being? From the modest beginnings of Small Heath Alliance to the Blue army of the modern era, here are the significant calling posts on a colourful journey through history . . .

1875

Formed in September as Small Heath Alliance by **a group of young cricketers** from Holy Trinity church, Bordesley Green. Played their first match in November, a **1-1 draw** against Holte Wanderers on wasteland at Arthur Street.

1876

The club moved to their first enclosed ground in Ladypool Road, Sparkbrook, with a capacity of about 3,000.

'The pitch became famous for its bumps and lack of grass'

1879

Small Heath defeated **Aston Villa 1-0** in a friendly match at Muntz Street. This was the **first meeting** between the two clubs.

1877

The club, growing in stature, moved to **Muntz Street**, Small Heath, on September 11. The ground was rented initially for **£5 a year**. The pitch became famous for its bumps and lack of grass.

1885

The club turned professional in August, becoming probably the first English team to do so. The players were initially not well paid but it was enough for most members of the squad to become professional footballers.

1886

Small Heath reached the **FA Cup semi-final**, losing 4-0 to West Bromwich Albion.

1875

1881

Small Heath first competed in the FA Cup.

1888

The club became a limited liability company on July 24, with a share capital of **£650.** They dropped the 'Alliance' from their name and became known as **Small Heath FC.**

1889

Small Heath were elected to become founder members of the Football Alliance, which was unofficially the Second Division.

1893

Small Heath became the first champions of the Second Division, scoring 90 goals in 22 matches, but they failed to gain promotion, losing to Newton Heath (later to become Manchester United) in a test match.

1890

Small Heath were **disqualified** from the FA Cup for fielding an **ineligible player.** Birmingham had already won two matches in the competition before the oversight was revealed.

1894

Small Heath **gained promotion** after finishing second in the Second Division, by defeating Darwen in a **test match** in Stoke. More than 1,000 people were waiting at **New Street Station** to cheer the train containing the Small Heath players.

'More than 1,000 people were waiting at New Street Station ...'

1895

Small Heath acquired the lease to Muntz Street, which had 11 years remaining, for a fee of £275.

1892

Small Heath became founder members of the Football League Second Division.

1895

1896

Small Heath were **relegated back** to the **Second Division.**

1897

Small Heath purchased a stand from Aston Villa, **at a cost of £90, and placed it behind one of the goals at** Muntz Street. **Even during Victorian times,** spectator comfort **was a** priority **in football.**

'Spectator comfort was a priority'

1903

Small Heath gained promotion back to the First Division. They were quickly acquiring a reputation **for being a 'yo-yo' club.**

1901

Small Heath finished as **runners-up** in the Second Division, **gaining promotion** back to the top flight.

1905

Small Heath finished seventh in the First Division. They also defeated Aston Villa for the first time in a league match. In March, the club changed its name to Birmingham FC. Harold Morris suggested to directors that the club move from Muntz Street to a new ground on Garrison Lane. The directors backed his plan and he sought new premises in the area.

1906

Birmingham signed a 21-year lease **on the new site. When the work was complete, the ground became known as** St Andrew's. **The cost of construction was** £10,000 **and the capacity was** reportedly 75,000, **although this was never put to the test.**

1896

1902

Small Heath were relegated back to the Second Division.

1907

St Andrew's **staged the FA Cup semi-final** between Woolwich Arsenal and Sheffield Wednesday. Wednesday won 3-1. Birmingham **made more than £1,000** for staging the match, despite having to make **significant alterations** to St Andrew's.

1908

Birmingham were relegated to the Second Division.

1913

Birmingham tour Denmark, their first foreign trip as a club. The Spion Kop at St Andrew's benefited from a new roof. Prior to that, it was uncovered. Frank Womack, **the Birmingham captain, was** offered a bribe **to fix the match at St Andrew's against Grimsby Town. He** reported the offer **to club officials who, in turn, informed the police. Birmingham lost 2-1.**

1910

Birmingham **finished bottom** of the Second Division but successfully **applied for re-election. Bob McRoberts** became the club's **first manager.** Prior to this, the team was selected by a committee.

''Frank Richards forgot to send in the application forms'

1920

Birmingham **did not enter** the FA Cup for the only time since 1881. **Frank Richards** forgot to send in the application forms.

1921

Birmingham acquired the freehold of St Andrew's **for about £7,000. Birmingham won the** Second Division championship.

1915

Frank Richards took over as secretary-manager.

1921

13

1923

William Beer **took over** as manager.

'Real Madrid lost 3-0 to Birmingham in a "challenge match" at St Andrew's'

1925

Real Madrid **lost 3-0 to Birmingham in a** "challenge match" **at St Andrew's. This was the** first time **a foreign team played at** St Andrew's.

1931

Birmingham reached the FA Cup final **for the** first time **but they lost 2-1 to West Bromwich Albion at** Wembley.

1928

Leslie **Knighton** took over as manager.

1933

George Liddell was **appointed manager**. Harry Morris junior, son of Harold Morris, **became chairman.**

1938

The first roofs **were placed above the** Tilton Road **stand and the** Railway End.

1923

1927

Bill Harvey took over as manager.

Birmingham City and Sparta Prague line up before a friendly at St Andrew's in 1947

1939

Birmingham's **record attendance**. A crowd of **67,341** turned up for the fifth round FA Cup tie **against Everton**, which ended 2-2. Birmingham were **relegated** to the Second Division. The police **closed down St Andrew's** because of the start of the **Second World War** - the threat of bomb damage deeming the **stadium unsafe**.

1941

The first international match at St Andrew's. England defeated Wales 2-1, although the match took place in wartime and does not count as an official international.

'Attempts to douse the flames... failed when a member of the fire service used petrol instead of water'

1942

The Main Stand was destroyed by fire. Attempts **to douse the** flames **sadly and, some would say, comically, failed when a** member of **the fire service** used petrol **instead of** water. Aston Villa offered Birmingham **the use of Villa Park**.

1943

Birmingham returned to **St Andrew's** but the dressing rooms were still unusable. The **players** were forced to change in a **factory nearby**. But wartime **matches** were still only glorified **friendlies**.

1940

St Andrew's was re-opened after an appeal by the Birmingham City Council.

1943

1945

Birmingham changed their name to Birmingham City on July 1. Edward Goodier was appointed caretaker-manager. Harry Storer became manager.

1946

Birmingham City won the Football League South Division (wartime) and also reached the FA Cup semi-finals. A new roof was placed over the Spion Kop and a new stand was erected on the Garrison Lane side.

1948

Birmingham City won the Second Division championship.

'Birmingham changed their name to Birmingham City . . .'

1950

Birmingham City were relegated to the Second Division.

1951

Birmingham lost in the FA Cup semi-final.

1945

1949

Bob Brocklebank (above) became the manager.

1954

The **Main Stand,** which would see Birmingham through to the end of the century, **was built.** In those days, it seemed **ahead of its time.** Arthur **Turner** was **appointed** manager.

1955

Birmingham won **the Second Division** championship **and were awarded a place in the Inter-cities** Fairs Cup, **a new** competition **for the clubs of European cities.**

1956

Birmingham's most **successful season.** They lost in the **FA Cup final (right)** at Wembley to Manchester City and **finished sixth in the First Division.** Floodlights were installed at **St Andrew's** for the first time. **Borussia Dortmund** were invited to play Birmingham to **celebrate the new lights.** The teams **drew 3-3.**

'In those days, it seemed ahead of its time'

1960

Gil **Merrick** was appointed **manager.** Birmingham reached the **final** of the Inter-cities **Fairs Cup,** losing to **Barcelona** of Spain over two legs.

1961

Birmingham again lost in **the Inter-cities Fairs Cup** final, **this time 4-2 on aggregate to** AS Roma **of Italy.**

1957

Birmingham lost in the FA Cup semi-finals.

1961

1963

Birmingham won the League Cup by defeating Aston Villa 3-1 on aggregate. The City Stand was built at the Railway End of the ground, turning St Andrew's into one of the most inspiring stadiums in the country.

1965

Stan Cullis (above, left in picture) was appointed manager. Birmingham were relegated to the Second Division.

'...turning St Andrew's into one of the most inspiring stadiums in the country'

1967

Birmingham lost in the League Cup semi-finals and also in the final of the FA Youth Cup.

1963

1964 Joe Mallett becomes manager.

'The distinctive globe badge, the **winning entry** of the competition... was introduced'

1975

Birmingham **lost** in the FA Cup **semi-finals.** Willie **Bell took over** originally as caretaker-manager.

1970

Fred **Goodwin (above, right in picture)** took over as **manager.** Trevor **Francis** made his Birmingham **debut,** aged just **16.**

1972

Birmingham **were** promoted **to the** First Division **and lost in the** FA Cup semi-finals. **The distinctive** globe badge, **the winning entry of a competition organised by the** Sports Argus, **was introduced.**

1968

Birmingham lost in the FA Cup semi-finals.

1975

1976

Executive boxes were added to the Main Stand.

1977

Sir Alf Ramsey, who led England to victory in the 1966 World Cup final, took over as manager.

1978

Jim Smith took over as manager after Ramsey resigned because of ill health.

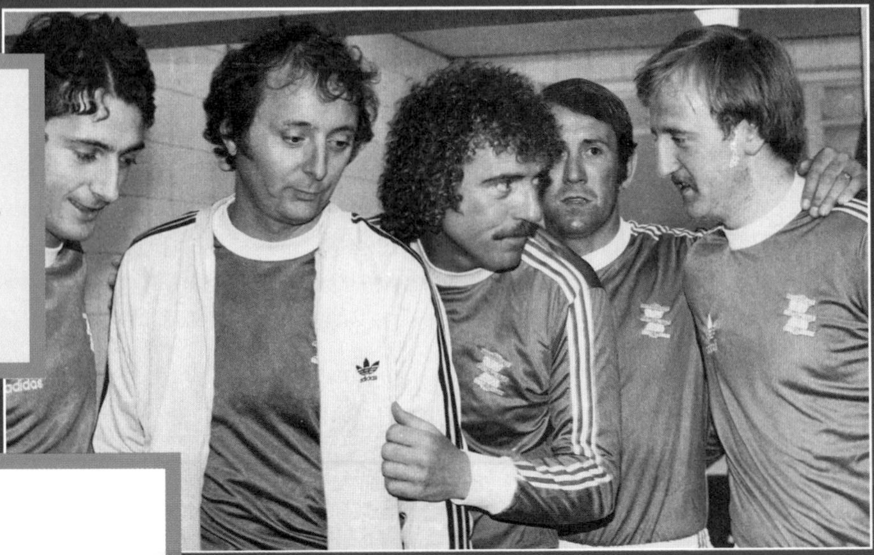

1979

Birmingham were relegated to the Second Division. Trevor Francis was sold to Nottingham Forest for £975,000, although the transfer was revealed to the media as being the first £1m deal in British football history. Robert Davies, more commonly known as Jasper Carrott (above, second left in picture), joined the board of directors.

'...the transfer was revealed to the media as being the first £1m deal in British football'

1982

Ron Saunders, the former Aston Villa manager, took over from Jim Smith.

1976

1980

Birmingham were promoted to the First Division.

Manager Ron Saunders celebrates promotion to the First Division in 1985

1984

Birmingham are relegated **to the Second Division.**

1985

The St Andrew's **riot. A young boy was killed when a wall collapsed.** Blues are promoted **to the First Division (above, right).**

1986

Birmingham were relegated to the **Second Division.** John Bond became the **manager.** Keith **Coombes resigned** as chairman, being replaced by **Ken Wheldon. The club revealed severe debts.**

'The money raised...did much to ensure that Birmingham did not go bankrupt'

1988

Birmingham **sold their Elmdon training ground for £350,000** plus **30 per cent** of re-development profits. The **money raised** from this sale did much to **ensure** that Birmingham did not go **bankrupt.**

1989

Birmingham were relegated **to the** Third Division **for the** first time. **Ken** Wheldon **sold his controlling interest in Birmingham to the** Kumar brothers **for £1.6m. Dave** Mackay **was appointed** manager.

1987 Garry Pendrey became manager.

1989

1991

Birmingham **won** the Leyland DAF Trophy **at Wembley.** Lou **Macari,** Bill **Coldwell** and Terry **Cooper** all had **spells as manager** of the club.

'St Andrew's became an all-seat stadium for the first time'

1992

Birmingham were promoted from the Third Division. **With the formation of the FA Premier League, Birmingham were** given a place **in the** new First Division. **Jack** Wiseman became chairman **after the textile business of the** Kumar brothers **was placed in the hands of receivers.**

1994

Birmingham endured relegation **to the Second Division. St Andrew's benefited from a** dramatic refurbishment **that cost nearly £8m. In keeping with the safety-first climate,** St Andrew's **became an** all-seat stadium **for the first time. Only the Main Stand, now old and dirty,** looked out of place.

STRICTLY PLAYERS & OFFICIALS ONLY

1993

The **most pivotal year** in Birmingham's history. David **Gold,** Ralph **Gold** and David **Sullivan bought the club** for £1.7m. Karren Brady was appointed **managing director.** Barry Fry was later appointed **manager.**

1995

Birmingham **won** the Second Division **championship** to claim promotion to the **First Division.** They also **won** the Auto Windscreens Shield **at Wembley.**

1999

A new stand **at the Railway End, which** cost nearly £5m, **was opened. Birmingham lost in the** play-off semi-finals **to Watford** on penalties.

1991

1996 Birmingham reached the semi-finals of the League Cup. Trevor Francis became the manager.

2002

Bruce's **effect was immediate.** Birmingham **secured promotion** to the **Premier League** after **defeating Norwich City** on penalties in the play-off final at Cardiff's **Millennium Stadium** (right).

2003

The arrival of Christophe Dugarry in January eased **Birmingham's** relegation fears. **They finished 13th, becoming the** highest-placed Midlands team **for the first time since 1906. Birmingham broke their** transfer record **to sign** David Dunn **from Blackburn Rovers for £5.5m.**

2001

Birmingham lost to Liverpool **on penalties** in the final **of the** League Cup **in Cardiff (right). Again, they** lost **in the** play-off semi-finals, **this time to Preston North End. Trevor** Francis resigned **in November. Steve** Bruce took over **as manager in December.**

2005

The **departure** of **Robbie Savage,** the midfield player who joined Blackburn Rovers, had **far-reaching consequences.** Birmingham were **never the same** after that and **slipped** into decline.

'Bruce's effect was immediate'

2000

Birmingham **again lost** in the **play-off semi-finals,** this time to Barnsley.

2006

Birmingham endured relegation **(left) to the Championship after crumbling from February. The** 7-0 defeat **to Liverpool in March, although taking place in the** sixth round of the FA Cup, **summed up their condition. Birmingham celebrated** 100 years **of life at** St Andrew's.

2004

Birmingham broke their transfer record again, this time to sign Emile Heskey from Liverpool for £6.5m.

2006

ere general. They occupied twelfth posi
eague table in the following season. In the
team went all to pieces; indeed, some of t
were little less than discreditable. Fourth

[kes, West Bromwich]

THE HOME OF BIRMINGHA

nd enterprise of the officials controlling the Birmingha
The playing field is well cared for, and the splendid te
Small Heath C

in of the gate ; the Football Association took
son expenses were, of course, correspondingly s
per- that professionalism was introduced, Small
tion £70 14s. 9d. in wages.

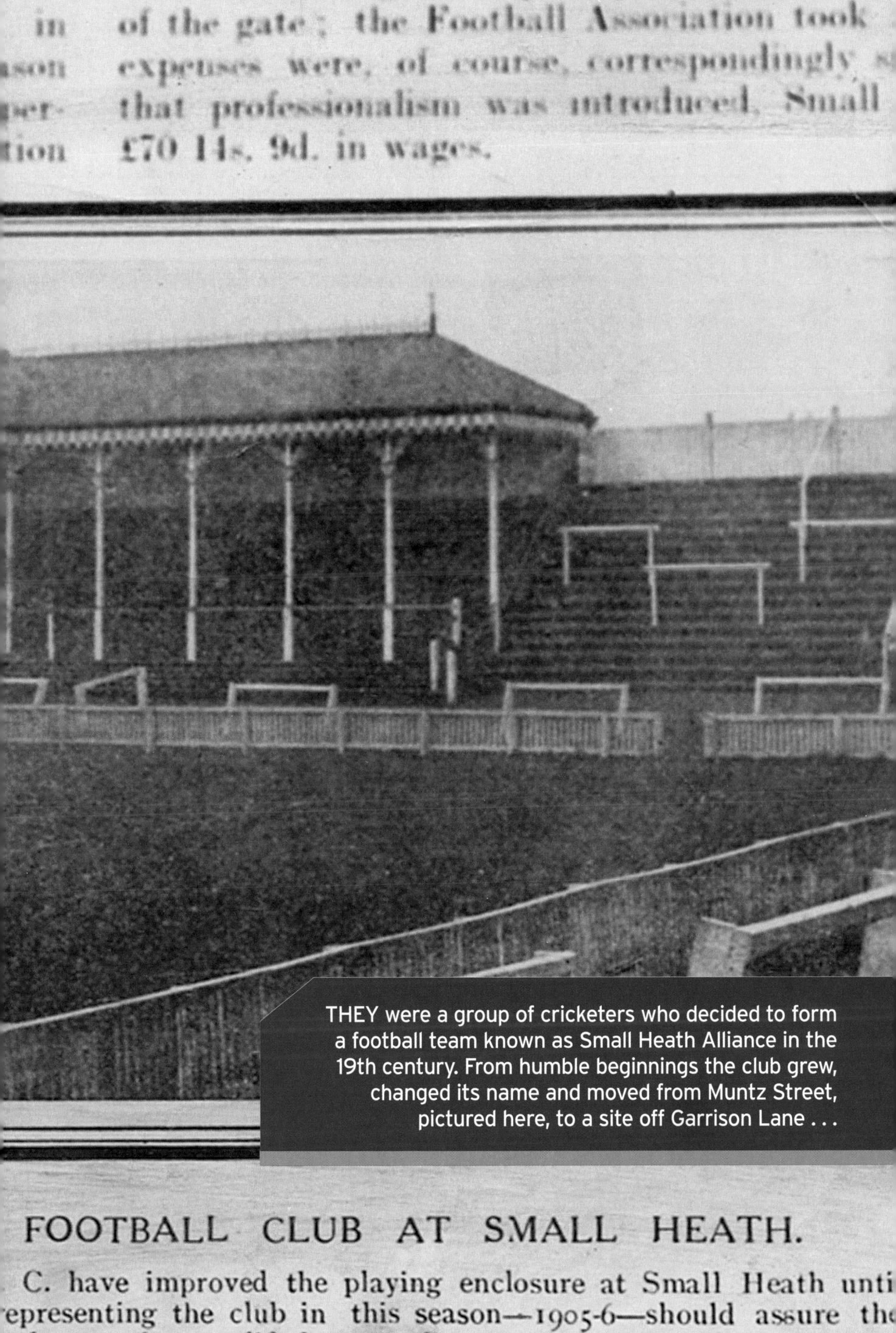

THEY were a group of cricketers who decided to form a football team known as Small Heath Alliance in the 19th century. From humble beginnings the club grew, changed its name and moved from Muntz Street, pictured here, to a site off Garrison Lane . . .

FOOTBALL CLUB AT SMALL HEATH.

C. have improved the playing enclosure at Small Heath unti
representing the club in this season—1905-6—should assure th
future of unqualified prosperity.

September 1875. Queen Victoria is at the helm of the British Empire. Ulysses Grant has strengthened links between the United States and the Hawaiian Islands. Russia is existing uneasily under Tsar Alexander II. Japan is moving swiftly into the modern world. And George Green has just patented the electric dental drill.

In Birmingham, with its population of nearly half a million people, a group of cricketers from the Holy Trinity Church formed a football club called Small Heath Alliance. The pioneers of the club are the three Edden brothers (Will, George and Thomas), the three James brothers (Arthur, Fred, and Tom) and William Edmunds. In such a male-dominated environment, a female managing director is inconceivable. In such a Protestant environment, a Jewish chairman is equally inconceivable. In such a working-class environment, a millionaire footballer is beyond the realms of possibility.

September 1875. This was a simple world, where setting up a football club was no more difficult than gathering together 11 players, a ball and a piece of land. Small Heath Alliance acquired some wasteland in Arthur Street, Bordesley, and played their first match that November against Holte Wanderers, a team from Aston in the north of the city. The match, which was, curiously, a 12-a-side affair, finished 1-1. David Keys scored Small Heath's goal and thus engraved his name forever into the history books.

Interest grew and, by 1877, the wasteland at Arthur Street was deemed inappropriate. Small Heath moved to Ladybrook Road in Sparkbrook, an enclosed ground with a capacity of about 3,000 spectators. There was no professional football but enthusiasm for this relatively new sport was uncontrollable. By the end of the year, Small Heath moved again, this time to Muntz Street at an annual rent of £5. It was around this time that the club was nicknamed the Heathens. They would remain at Muntz Street, attracting more interest, turning professional in the process, for 29 years. The problem (if, indeed, it was a problem) was that Small Heath were far too good for their opponents. They played 22 matches during the 1877-78 campaign and remained undefeated. Arthur James was their most prominent player. He represented the Birmingham Association representative team and acquired the nickname of 'People's Pet'. William Edmunds, who played in the club's first match, became the club's first honorary secretary. Later, Will Edden, who appeared in goal in Small Heath's first match, became secretary.

Four years after their formation, on September 27, 1879, they welcomed to Muntz Street a club that was growing significantly in reputation. This match between Small Heath and Aston Villa was the first of what was to become the greatest rivalry in Midlands football. Small Heath won 1-0 but the match attracted little attention.

It was around about this time that Muntz Street gained a reputation for its bumpy, unforgiving pitch. When Small Heath were drawn at home to play Wednesbury Old Athletic in the Walsall Cup in 1882-83, they were offered a gift of five guineas to switch the tie to Wednesbury's ground. Wednesbury could not stomach the prospect of playing at Muntz Street but the switch did not help them - Small Heath won 4-1 and, towards the end of the season, won the Walsall Cup. This was the club's first trophy.

Birmingham turned professional in August 1885, probably the first in England to do so and their first 'star' player became Harold Morris, who was a teenager then, and who would later decide that Small Heath should move to St Andrew's.

But that was 20 years in the future. For now, winning football matches was more important than building a new stadium. And Small Heath had fashioned a talented team, which reached the FA Cup semi-final in 1886. Unfortunately, they lost 4-0 to West Bromwich Albion.

In July 1888, just weeks before the start of the new Football League, Small Heath Alliance changed their name to Small Heath FC and became the first club to appoint a board of directors. The first chairman was Walter Hart, who, in his first year, was able to report that the club made a healthy profit and would pay a five per cent dividend. A move into the Football Alliance, then the most powerful league outside the Football League itself, was inevitable but the increased competition made life awkward for Small Heath.

These were not good times for the club, although they boasted, in Will and Ted Devey, two members of five brothers who became famous in the city. The other three brothers played for Aston Villa. Will Devey was the Small Heath captain from 1888-91 and earned 12s 6d (60 pence) per week, which was above the national average for a 'working' man.

Small Heath improved by 1891-92 and, along with most members of the Football Alliance, they were invited to

Lifting the Birmingham Senior Cup following victory over Aston Villa in 1983 - 78 years after first winning it as Small Heath

form the Football League Second Division in 1892. The timing was perfect. Small Heath scored 90 goals in 22 matches and won the title. But, although they could claim to be one of the top 25 teams in Britain (and, therefore, the world), they were not granted a place in the First Division. In those days, even the champions had to take part in a test match - now known as the play-offs -and Small Heath lost a replay 5-2 to Newton Heath (later to be called Manchester United) in Sheffield.

Small Heath finished runners-up in the Second Division in 1894 and this time gained promotion to the First

Division by defeating Darwen in the test match in Stoke. When the players returned, on a train painted in the club colours of royal blue to mark the victory, more than 1,000 Small Heath supporters waited at New Street train station to show their approval.

Attendances at Muntz Street in the First Division averaged 6,400 - more than twice the average of their matches in the Second Division the previous season. But Small Heath were not of the required First Division standard. They avoided relegation by winning their final match of the 1894-95 season but were relegated to the Second

Division in 1896. Interest waned and attendances slipped back towards the 2,000-mark - hardly enough to attract prominent players on a consistent level. One good player who did sign for Small Heath was Alex Leake, who would later join Aston Villa and play for England.

In 1897, Birmingham and Aston Villa were friendly enough to conduct an interesting piece of business. It did not involve a player, but a stand, which was transferred from Villa's old ground at Perry Barr to behind a goal at Muntz Street.

It was not long before Small Heath

In 1904-05, Small Heath were at their peak. They finished seventh in the First Division and won three local trophies - the Lord Mayor Cup, the Birmingham Senior Cup and the Staffordshire Senior Cup.

In view of the improvement, and the certainty that Small Heath was the largest club in the city of Birmingham, there was only one logical conclusion: Small Heath as a name was no longer appropriate.

In March 1905, at a dinner for the players at the Swan Hotel in Yardley, it was agreed that Small Heath should change its name to Birmingham FC. The original proposal of Thomas Todd, a director, was for the club to be called Birmingham City.

The shareholders did not like the 'City' bit and opted just for Birmingham. The name change turned a provincial club into a national one.

On September 16, 1905, the club defeated Aston Villa for the first time. More than 32,000 were in attendance at Muntz Street and this was perhaps the first time that Birmingham were considered superior to Villa.

The next step was just as significant.

Street.

It was not long before Small Heath improved and they scored 35 goals in four matches. They defeated Chirk 8-0 in the FA Cup, Luton Town 9-0 in the Second Division, Druids 10-0 in the FA Cup and Darwen 8-0 in the Second Division.

It was not until the turn of the century, however, that Small Heath became bankable again. They returned to the First Division in 1901 after finishing runners-up in the Second Division.

They endured relegation in 1902 and gained promotion back to the First Division in 1903. That was when Harold Morris retired from playing and became a club director. It was significant, for Morris was a man of vision.

Above: Goalkeeper Gil Merrick dives at the feet of a Manchester City player during the 1956 FA Cup final at Wembley. Below: Trevor Francis heads a derby winner in 1976

With Muntz Street struggling to cope with the dramatic change in Birmingham's fortunes, Harold Morris stepped forward to convince club directors that a move was necessary.

Today, even the most biased of Birmingham City supporters would admit that St Andrew's has never been aesthetically pleasing.

But, in one sense, the lack of architectural style - St Andrew's has never been more than functional - has helped to give the stadium savage appeal.

If atmosphere is more important than comfort, this is the place to be. Even in these times of all-seat stadiums, where attendances are lower than they were in the early post-War years, and where crowd participation is diminished, the spirit at St Andrew's is unique.

Cut like a canyon into endless rows of terraced houses, St Andrew's seems to evoke merged images of the uncomplicated past and the sophisticated present. Few stadiums in England can provide such conflicting emotions.

In the early years of the Edwardian period, football stadiums were cheap and humble creations that paid little attention to safety or luxury.

It was all about packing in as many working-class people as possible. The middle classes were, largely, more interested in cricket and lawn tennis. Football was for the proletariat. Football was for those who did not mind being wet or cold on a Saturday afternoon.

Interesting, then, that one middle-class gentleman - Morris, a former player and chairman - chanced upon "a wilderness of stagnant water and muddy slopes" off Garrison Lane,

The current St Andrew's - home of the club formerly known as Small Heath

Bordesley Green, and saw the future home of Birmingham FC. This was 1905. The club had only just changed its name from Small Heath FC and were still playing at Muntz Street, near to Coventry Road.

Muntz Street, which could house up to 30,000 people in discomfort, and had been the club's home since 1877, was archaic and had no place in the 20th century.

It was easier to climb over the fence than it was to pay at the gates. The pitch was bumpy and the overall impression was one of a small club, not one that essentially represented the growing metropolis of Birmingham.

Walter Hart, the Birmingham chairman, backed Morris and the club launched a debenture scheme that raised enough money to acquire the land off Garrison Lane.

In February 1906, the land was acquired on a 21-year lease at what was described as "advantageous terms".

Turning the wilderness of mud and water into a football ground required much work and fortitude.

Providing a name was easier.

The ground sat uneasily on St Andrew's Street and made the decision simple.

St Andrew's was about to enter football parlance.

THE topsy-turvy nature of Birmingham City's progress once they had decamped to St Andrew's could perhaps finally be explained, as a group of travellers leave their mark on the Garrison Road site. All eyes on the corners of the pitch . . .

For such a famous team representing such a large metropolis, Birmingham City has been surprisingly fruitless. In terms of significant success, they can only point to the League Cup which they won in 1963, and even that was at a time when the competition was ignored by the larger clubs.

To more fanciful supporters, the lack of prosperity goes back to 1906, when Birmingham acquired land at Garrison Lane and called it St Andrew's.

Legend has it that the site was once occupied by gypsies and, unable to accept that a football club could use the premises for matches, placed a curse on the team. The stories go that, when Birmingham began to build St Andrew's, they forced a group of travellers off the land.

If there has been a curse, it seems to have survived for a century. During the 2005-06 season, Birmingham performed poorly at St Andrew's. The nadir came in March when Birmingham lost 7-0 at home to Liverpool in the sixth round of the FA Cup. During 2005, a tornado that struck the nearby suburb of Moseley caused slight damage to St Andrew's.

More than a decade before, when Birmingham were flirting with chronic failure, there were stories, probably apocryphal, that the club was taking extreme measures to rid St Andrew's of the so-called curse.

Barry Fry, then the manager, claimed to have urinated in all four corners of the pitch, although this was probably a publicity stunt.

In the 1980s, Ron Saunders is said to have had crosses placed on the floodlights and had the soles of his players' boots painted red, to ward off the effect of the curse.

Barry Fry - did he do his bit to banish the curse from St Andrew's?

International line-up: Johnny Crosbie (Scotland), Stan Davies (Wales) and Joe Bradford (England) in training, circa 1928

Whatever the reasons (and nobody can seriously suggest that a gypsy's curse is to blame), the fact is inescapable: Birmingham City are the greatest underachievers in English football. And yet, the bond that the club has with its supporters marks it out as unique. The club draws its support from a relatively small catchment area. If Aston Villa is said to be the 'regional' club, Birmingham is certainly the 'city' club. But supporting Birmingham is not easy. It never has been. You do it because your heart tells you to do it.

That has been the case since the club changed its name from Small Heath to Birmingham in March 1905. In those days, the club was the only one in the Football League to be located within the boundaries of the city, and so the name-change was seen as appropriate. Now, supporters could identify with a club that effectively represented the city.

Alas, the history of Birmingham City FC is one of frustration, sweat and tears, with only fragments of contentment in between.

The period from 1905 to the beginning of the First World War was one of monotony. They slipped into the Second Division and did not come close to promotion until the outbreak of hostilities. The FA Cup provided little relief.

When football restarted after the War in 1919, Birmingham were one of the few clubs to benefit from the break. With Harry Hampton and Jack Jones in the team, Birmingham came close to gaining promotion in 1920, finishing third behind Tottenham Hotspur and

Birmingham City team photograph, circa 1956

Huddersfield Town. It was in 1919 that Dan Tremelling, the former Lincoln City goalkeeper, made his debut for Birmingham.

He would remain at St Andrew's until 1931, making 395 appearances (Tremelling once denied Cardiff City the League Championship. On the final day of the 1923-24 season, the goalkeeper saved a penalty by Len Davies, meaning that Cardiff only drew with Birmingham, handing the title to Huddersfield Town). He was replaced by Harry Hibbs, who made 388 appearances until 1939, who in turn was replaced by Gil Merrick, who played 551 matches for Birmingham

until 1960. All three played for England.

Birmingham failed to enter the FA Cup in 1920-21 when Sam Richards, the club secretary, forgot to send in the application form. "It was just one of those things," he said, but the players eased his guilt by gaining promotion to the First Division at the end of the season. Having Joe Bradford in the team helped. Here was a striker of style, pace and composure. He served Birmingham well from 1921 to 1935. Attendances at St Andrew's also boomed that year. The average of more than 31,000 was a reflection of Birmingham's exciting play.

Life in the First Division was tougher, however, and Birmingham tended to finish in the bottom half of the table, without ever suggesting that they would endure relegation. They remained in the top flight until the final day of the 1938-39 season when they finished in 21st position and thus suffered relegation.

In the FA Cup, they showed improvement. With Leslie Knighton as manager, they reached the final in 1931, 50 years after first entering the competition. Although Birmingham were in the First Division and Albion in the Second, it was Albion who were favourites to win the final. Birmingham had finished 19th in the top flight and only avoided relegation because they won their final two matches of the season. Albion, meanwhile, were about to secure promotion and were on the rise. Worst of all for Birmingham, their most important player, Joe Bradford, had suffered a knee injury in the run-up to the match and only declared himself fit after breakfast on the morning of the final. Heavy rain turned the Wembley pitch into a mud bath and Birmingham were short of their best. Bradford did score but Albion won 2-1 with a late winner.

Scoring goals was Birmingham's problem throughout the inter-War period and they might have slipped out of the top flight long before they did but for the form of Hibbs in goal. For a

time, it was probably that Hibbs was the best goalkeeper in the world. It did not help that Knighton resigned to become manager of Chelsea in 1933. Birmingham appointed George Liddell, a former Birmingham player, but the team were in decline. Birmingham avoided relegation by one point in 1934 but it was obvious that they would be found out eventually. Liddell used 70 players during his six years in charge but he left five months after Birmingham endured relegation to the Second Division in 1939 (incidentally Birmingham had reached the fifth round of the FA Cup and their match against Everton attracted a crowd of 67,341 to St Andrew's, a record for the stadium. But Birmingham lost in a replay).

The 1939-40 season lasted just three matches. The Second World War began on September 3. Competitive football did not return until 1945, with the FA Cup, and league football did not return until 1946. By then Birmingham had changed their name to Birmingham City and began the process of rebuilding St Andrew's after a fire destroyed the Main Stand during the War. Worse still, the German Luftwaffe scored at least 20 direct hits on the ground during the War years. This led to all home games being played at Villa Park.

Birmingham supporters would have been forgiven for thinking that there was, in fact, a gypsy's curse at St Andrew's. When the club celebrated its 70th anniversary in September 1945, St

Noel Kinsey shoots Birmingham City level in the 1956 FA Cup final against Manchester City

A groundsman clears the snow from the St Andrew's pitch while the players train on the track ahead of the FA Cup tie against Lincoln City in 1969

Andrew's was crumbling and Birmingham had still not won anything that constituted significant success. But the new name and a new manager, Harry Storer, provided optimism at St Andrew's. Within 10 years, St Andrew's would be refurbished and Birmingham City would be among the best teams in Britain.

In 1946, Birmingham won the Football League Championship South and reached the FA Cup semi-finals. In the three seasons after the War, Birmingham were defeated only eight times at St Andrew's in 63 matches, conceding only 102 goals in 126 games. They also won the Second Division championship in 1948.

The 1954-55 season saw Birmingham, under Arthur Turner, gain promotion from the Second Division to the First Division, hastening a period of prosperity that set the standard for future managers and teams. But the title success was a close-run thing. Birmingham edged Luton Town into second spot, taking the title by just 0.297 of a goal. Turner produced perhaps the best team to play at St Andrew's and during that promotion season Birmingham scored 92 league goals, with four strikers finishing with double figures. The season after, Birmingham reached the FA Cup final, losing 3-1 to Manchester City at Wembley.

In 1956, Birmingham became the first English club to play in Europe, playing in the Inter-cities Fairs Cup.

They would reach the final twice, losing on each occasion to Barcelona in 1960 and AS Roma in 1961. But Birmingham, whose FA Cup tie at home to Bury in 1963 was postponed 14 times, were in decline. They did win the League Cup in 1963, defeating Aston Villa over two legs, but that was in the days before the winners were given a place in Europe. Most of the more successful clubs avoided the competition and the achievement was not as great as it would have been from the late Sixties onwards. Still, this triumph makes Gil Merrick the most successful manager in the club's history.

He was also one of the club's finest players, turning himself into a goalkeeper of international standard.

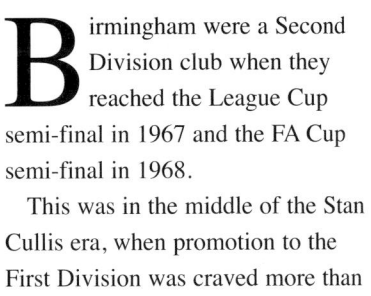

Birmingham were a Second Division club when they reached the League Cup semi-final in 1967 and the FA Cup semi-final in 1968.

This was in the middle of the Stan Cullis era, when promotion to the First Division was craved more than anything else.

It would take the departure of Cullis in 1970 and the arrival of Freddie Goodwin before Birmingham could realise their top-flight ambitions.

The Sixties did not swing at St Andrew's.

But the Seventies would.

Above, top: Blues go close against Southampton, 1960s. Above: New Blues manager Freddie Goodwin introduces himself to the players soon after they reported back to Elmdon training ground, 1970. Goodwin would soon deliver First Division football to St Andrew's

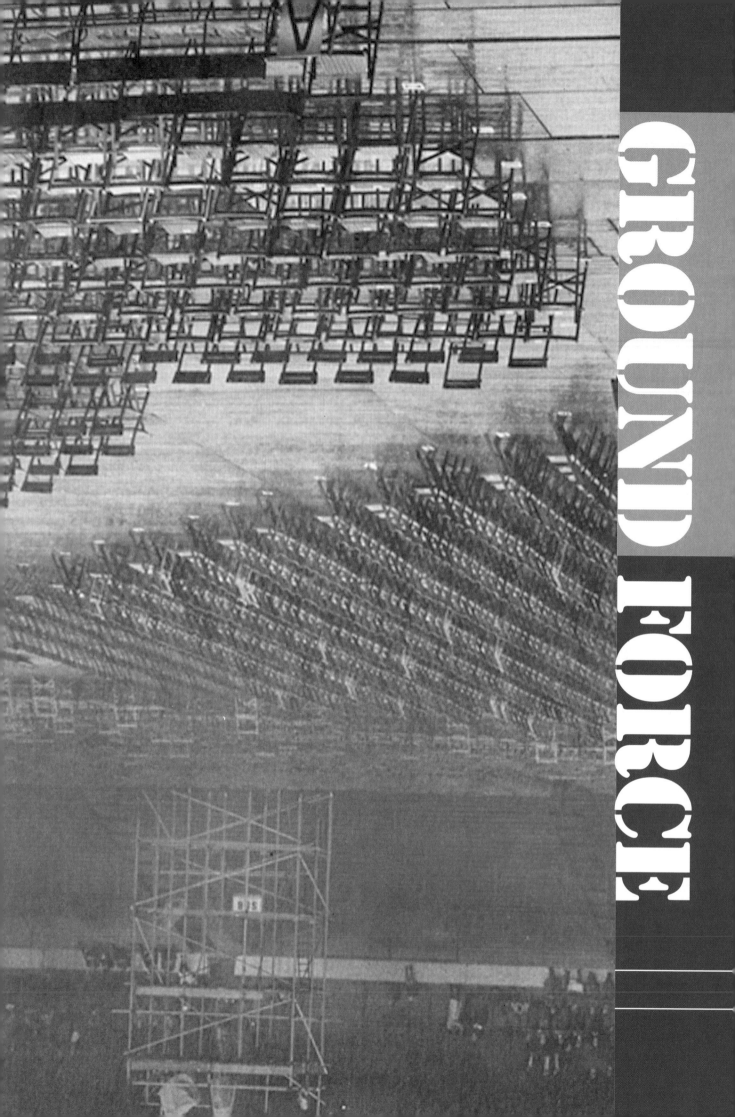

GROUND FORCE

PRIZE fights and big football nights. The history of St Andrew's - from humble beginnings off Garrison Lane to a 75,000-capacity ground (via this spell as host for a boxing match, circa 1950), to its current form as a 30,000 all-seater arena. There's no place like home . . .

It is in keeping with the nature of Birmingham City's anomalous history that the club's most significant player only appeared for the club in one Football League match, and that was in 1893 when it was called Small Heath FC. Harold Morris was a footballer, a Birmingham director, a chairman, a plumber, a businessman and the father of a dynasty that remained a significant part of the club until the late Sixties.

Morris had joined the club as a player in 1884. By 1905, his horizon had widened, for it was his proposal that Small Heath FC, about to be renamed Birmingham FC, should move from the inadequate but much loved Muntz Street to a new ground nearby. Morris located "a wilderness of stagnant water and muddy slopes" just off Garrison Lane in Bordesley Green and visualised an arena that befitted a growing club like Birmingham.

Morris did not ask an architect to design the new stadium. That would have been too expensive. Instead, he approached Harry Pumfrey, a carpenter, to draw up plans for St Andrew's. With the help of volunteers, often working from breakfast until late into the evening, Birmingham saved something in the region of £2,000.

Clearing the expanse of mud was one thing; turning it into a football ground was quite another. Laying a pitch was one particularly difficult task, for much of the wasteland was covered in mud and artesian spring water. Two large pools of water needed to be drained and then the holes needed to be filled by tons of rubble. Thomas Turley headed up the operation, working alongside Pumfrey. In those days, when machinery was basic, it was remarkable that a team of volunteers could perform such a difficult task.

Eventually, more than 10,000 square yards of turf was laid and the pitch began to take shape. Based on the initial plans, the pitch was supposed to be the largest in the country. By June 1906, the pitch was evident but there was no sign of a stadium.

Building terraces - or banks as they were called in those days - was just as difficult as laying down a pitch. Inspired by the Spion Kop at Anfield in Liverpool, Birmingham wanted to build the largest Kop in the country. Whereas the Kop at Anfield was behind one of the goals, the Kop at St Andrew's hugged one of the touchlines. To build such a bank, Birmingham asked members of the public to dump their rubbish on what was to become known

The 'gap' at the back of the Main Stand at St Andrew's, noted by one Birmingham Post & Mail reader, pictured in January 1964

Taking cover at St Andrew's: First pioneered at Tottenham, two polythene covers (with a third to come, total cost £500) provide pitch protection, March 1961

as the "unreserved" side of the ground. Thousands of tons of rubbish was dumped there. In later years, when Aston Villa supporters metaphorically refer to St Andrew's as a rubbish tip, they are closer to the truth than they think. The St Andrew's Kop had no barriers or steps but, by the time it was finished, it was large enough to house 48,000 people.

The next plan was to erect a roof at the Tilton Road End "to protect at least 12,000 supporters from inclement weather". Then a grandstand was built at the opposite side to the Kop. Here, in 29 rows, was seating for more than 6,000 people, with additional room in front for a further 5,000 to stand - all under cover. The grandstand, soon to be called the Main Stand, was built using nearly half a million bricks, 40 tons of

corrugated iron, more than 100 tons of cement and a large quantity of timber.

Supporters were given a wide choice of ticket price, in six different sections. Prices ranged from one shilling to two shillings. They could access their seats from two staircases, which were illuminated by electric lights. The Main Stand was where the club built its offices. There were also refreshment rooms, the boardroom, a cycle store, a small training area for players, a billiard room, a large bath and, of course, the player's changing rooms.

When St Andrew's was completed in December 1906, after nearly a year of work and at a total cost of £10,000, the official capacity was recorded at 75,000. This was never tested but St Andrew's was among the largest

grounds in the country. Birmingham signed a 21-year lease for the ground, which occupied an area of nearly eight acres.

Next came the race against time. Birmingham wanted to officially open the ground in 1906 rather than wait until 1907. They pencilled in the match against Middlesbrough on December 26, to stage the opening ceremony. Only bad weather could spoil the party - and that was what nearly happened. When club officials woke up on that Boxing Day morning, they saw nothing but snow. The chances of the match taking place were diminishing by the hour.

With a large crowd expected, and various local politicians invited, Birmingham could not afford a postponement. Inevitably, dozens of

41

The newly opened 17 executive boxes at St Andrew's (costing fans £5000 for 3 years), August 1976

volunteers offered to clear the pitch and the embankments of snow. They were only partially successful - there was still an expanse of white everywhere - but the efforts were enough to ensure that the match took place. Birmingham produced a special programme for the occasion and Sir John Holder, a local millionaire, officially opened the stadium before 32,000-plus spectators. Somehow, the match had to be an anti-climax. Good football was impossible on the slippery surface and the goalless draw was inevitable.

There were only 20,000-plus present for the next match at St Andrew's, against Preston North End three days later. This time, with the snow long since melted, Birmingham won 3-0 and Ben Green became the first player to score at St Andrew's.

The Football Association was impressed with St Andrew's and the English game's governing body decided to stage one of the 1907 FA Cup semi-finals, Woolwich Arsenal against Sheffield Wednesday, at the stadium. Wednesday won 3-1 and Birmingham made more than £1,000 for staging the match, despite having to make significant alterations to St Andrew's.

The ground changed little for the next two decades, however, although Birmingham acquired the freehold of St Andrew's for about £7,000 in 1921. This ensured that the club were financially secure, for they no longer needed to pay rent and could develop the ground as they saw fit. It was 1939 before any significant improvements were made when the Railway End and the Tilton Road End were each given a roof. The roof at the Railway End was still evident until the early Nineties.

When Birmingham played Everton in an FA Cup fifth-round tie on February 11, 1939, a crowd of 67,341 was recorded. This remains Birmingham's record attendance and is unlikely to be beaten for as long as the club remains at St Andrew's. But the Second World War broke out in September 1939 and, soon after, St Andrew's was closed down by the local authorities because the threat of bombs made the ground unsafe. Birmingham appealed against the decision, played some of their home matches at Villa Park, and ensured that the matter was raised in Parliament. Birmingham's gripe was understandable, for St Andrew's was the only ground in the country to be closed down.

Eventually, the ban was lifted, but the issue left a nasty taste. With cruel irony, the Main Stand was destroyed by fire in January 1942. The stand was actually being used as a temporary fire station and some poor soul, in attempting to put out a brazier with what he thought was water, sprayed petrol all over the place, causing a devastating fire. Most significantly, the club's records, stretching back to 1875, perished in the fire and were lost forever.

Rebuilding the Main Stand took time

Snow ploughs battle to clear the St Andrew's pitch, circa 1982

Workmen spreading concrete on the Railway End terracing

and, having begun in 1952, was not actually completed until 1954. Floodlights were added in 1956 - Borussia Dortmund were invited to St Andrew's to embellish the party - and the early Sixties brought two European finals to the stadium when Birmingham played in the Inter-cities Fairs Cup. By then, a new roof was placed over the Tilton Road End and the Kop, while the club built a replica of the Main Stand at the Railway End. St Andrew's had entered the modern world and, by 1976, was even able to offer richer supporters executive boxes.

If St Andrew's was of its time in the mid-Seventies, it quickly began to look dated. By the early Nineties, when David Gold, Ralph Gold and David Sullivan bought the club, St Andrew's looked tired and in need of dramatic refurbishment. The work began quickly. In 1994, the terracing on the west and

east sides were removed and replaced with all-seat stands that each boasted a cantilever roof. In 2000, a two-tier stand was opened at the west end. By the time Steve Bruce took the club into the Premiership in 2002, St Andrew's was an all-seat stadium with a capacity of 30,018.

The St Andrew's of 2006 did not resemble the St Andrew's of 1906 but, through toil and circumstance, the stadium was able to reflect the fortunes of the team. However, two years before Birmingham were able to celebrate the 100th birthday of St Andrew's, on Tuesday, April 27, 2004, a story by Neil Connor appeared in The Birmingham Post.

'Birmingham City and Warwickshire County Cricket Club are in talks with council chiefs over proposals to move to a new 60,000-seat stadium planned for Birmingham's Eastside. The

proposed arena will be based on the design of Melbourne's Telstra Dome but will be more technologically advanced and will boast a fully retractable roof and moveable lower levels of seating. Athletics events will also be staged there.

'After months of speculation and denials, The Birmingham Post understands council leisure chiefs are set to commission a feasibility study into the project, which will provide a focal point of the city's emerging Eastside district and one of the most modern sports stadia in Europe.

'Birmingham City and Warwickshire are keen to leave their historic homes. Both have been beset with problems over ground improvements. As well as being the venue for Birmingham City and Warwickshire home games, the new stadium would have the benefit of being able to stage international cricket matches in summer and winter, as well as major athletics meetings.

'Leisure chiefs are keen to build on the city's sporting reputation after Birmingham was named the host city for the 2007 European Indoor Athletics Championships earlier this week, a year after the city successfully staged the world event.

'The new stadium would mean Birmingham would be in prime position to stage the World Outdoor Athletics Championships and, in the long term, the Commonwealth Games.'

The superstadium was the baby of Karren Brady, the club's visionary managing director, who became the public face of the bid and turned the project into her raison d'Ítre. She rose to the task, turning herself into an admirable spokesperson, a formidable worker and diplomatic politician. It seemed inconceivable that the bid would fail. Soon after, a model of the new stadium, and its surrounding areas, was placed in the reception area at St Andrew's. The irony was there for all to see, for the model looked like the future and St Andrew's looked like the past. Even the most sentimental of Birmingham supporters could see that St Andrew's had gone beyond its sell-by date. The future began here.

On the same day, The Birmingham Post backed the scheme with this comment piece:

'The future has finally caught up with Birmingham City. At some point over the next four years, they will vacate their bed-and-breakfast accommodation at St Andrew's, migrate to a luxury suite in Eastside, and make a momentous leap into the 21st century.

'The proposed 60,000-seat stadium, a clone of the Telstra Dome in

Captain Stan Harland with City chairman Clifford Coombes and the Lord Mayor Alderman Victor Turton, May 1972 with a joint Birmingham City and Aston Villa cake

Melbourne, will be everything that St Andrew's is not. It will provide Birmingham City with the means by which to develop their operation, improve their team, and challenge the elite of Europe.

'Football in the city may never be the same again. In taking such a bold step, Birmingham City are merely following convention.

'Manchester City have gone from Maine Road to Eastlands, Arsenal are set to leave Highbury for Ashburton Grove, and Liverpool are set to leave Anfield for New Anfield.

'Like sharks, healthy clubs move forwards; unhealthy ones stand still. Birmingham City are doing what any self-respecting businesses do: expanding wisely to meet the needs of a

An aerial picture taken of St Andrew's from 1986 (above). Below: A lone workman surveys the view from the new floodlights, being tested days before the first game under lights against Borussia Dortmund in 1956

growing customer base. Sentiment has no place in the real world of football. St Andrew's, which has served Birmingham City with little distinction since 1906, has never been regarded as a stadium for its time and has never looked comfortable with a makeover.

'At its best, it just about does the job; at its worst, it is an architectural monstrosity. Visiting supporters often mock St Andrew's but more significantly was the reaction of one Premiership player who, when asked this season if he was joining Birmingham City, said: "Only if they knock down the Main Stand." That has always been Birmingham City's problem. How do you convince the world that you are a big club when your stadium has all the hallmarks of the Football League?

'The perception that Aston Villa is the largest club in the city owes much to the quality of their Villa Park stadium. All that will surely change. When Eastside opens to facilitate a ground share between Birmingham City and Warwickshire County Cricket Club, the balance of power will shift away from Aston Villa.

'Suddenly, international matches and FA Cup semi-finals that might have gone to Villa Park will be offered to Eastside. Villa's response will certainly be to expand Villa Park, meaning that the punters - the people who matter most - will be the beneficiaries.

'There will be those Birmingham

An artist's impression of 'how the Railway End will look after £35,000 improvements have been made' in 1962 (above); how the stand looked as it neared completion, with seating for 2,600 spectators (opposite page, top)

City supporters who will not favour a move away from St Andrew's, but they are probably the same people whose great-grandfathers opposed the move from Muntz Street in 1906.

'The Telstra Dome is a technological work of art and, unlike St Andrew's, sets the pulse racing even when empty. I know. I ate a packet of crisps there two years ago.

'I am looking forward to doing the same at Eastside, by which time Birmingham City will have facilities to match clubs such as Manchester United, Boca Juniors, Benfica and Ajax.'

That was the dream. The reality, alas, was somewhat different. In The Birmingham Post on March 21, 2006, Paul Dale wrote this report:

'Birmingham City Council is out of the race for Britain's first super-casino - leaving Solihull with a clear run to campaign for an American-style gambling complex at the National Exhibition Centre.

'The council's Tory-Liberal Democrat leadership decided yesterday not to recommend Birmingham to the Government as the location for a regional casino with unlimited cash prizes.

'Instead, the cabinet threw its weight behind Solihull Council which is to submit a formal bid on behalf of the NEC. The decision put paid to Birmingham City Football Club's ambitious plan for a super-casino at Saltley, the income from which would have paid for a £120m 55,000-seat multi-sports stadium and new home for the Blues.

'Birmingham council leaders, with support from the Labour opposition, made it clear that they would seek a binding agreement with the NEC that money generated from a super-casino would be used to build a City of Birmingham Stadium capable of hosting a future Commonwealth Games.

'The NEC and American casino partners MGM claim a super-casino would create thousands of jobs and release £350m over 10 years for the city council, an income stream that could be used to pay for a variety of regeneration projects including the new stadium and a sports village.

'The NEC casino scheme attracted the support of many Birmingham-based business organisations. However, more than 20,000 people signed a petition urging the council to back the Birmingham City proposal. There have been claims by the football club that the council is too closely involved to make a rational decision, since it owns a controlling share in the NEC.

'Council leader Mike Whitby said the NEC proposal should be viewed as a

West Midlands project because it had the backing of five of the seven metropolitan councils. The cabinet was told by Stephen Hughes, the interim chief executive, that it faced a "stark" choice. If the cabinet wanted to support the NEC proposal, members had little option but to throw their weight behind Solihull, he argued.

'Putting in a bid for Birmingham and still supporting Solihull would not work, he said. Sir Albert Bore, leader of the Labour opposition group, said an NEC casino could help regenerate a large part of inner city Birmingham but

the council had to be clear in its objectives from the beginning.

"'If this council is to line up with Solihull we need to have some assurances that cannot be unpicked, that the benefits from a casino operation would be used to meet the objectives that we have all signed up for," he added.

"'The Government-appointed Casino Advisory Panel has given local authorities until the end of this month to declare an interest in hosting the first super-casino. Solihull, if chosen by the CAP, would have to invite applications

from interested parties raising the likelihood that the NEC proposal would not be the only bid to come forward.'"

Karren Brady's vision, though admirable, was not enough. Birmingham City's dream of moving to a new stadium was dependent on acquiring the rights to operate a super casino. Without the casino, there would be no new stadium. Without a new stadium, Birmingham would remain at St Andrew's for the time being. On December 26, 2006, St Andrew's entered its second century, still the home of Birmingham City.

A youngster shows how fans climb a broken wall overlooking the Railway End terrace to gain entrance to St Andrew's

The new railings to fence in the crowd at the Tilton Road End, used for the first time against Cardiff City in 1969 (above, top); the framework almost completed at the Railway End in 1961 (above, left); new turnstiles at the Coventry Road side (above, right)

Outside St Andrew's in June 1966 are (left to right): Alan Instone, club secretary; Moss Livingstone, supporters' club chairman; Denis Howell, Minister for Sport; Stan Cullis, manager and David Exall, administrative manager (above, left); the footprints suggest a sodden pitch at St Andrew's (above, right); members of the secretarial staff installed in the new offices under the new stand, November 1955 (below)

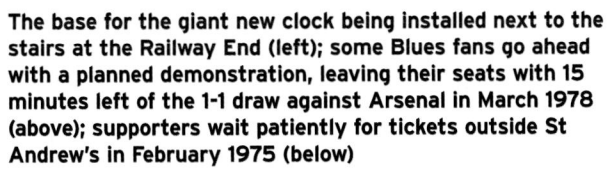

The base for the giant new clock being installed next to the stairs at the Railway End (left); some Blues fans go ahead with a planned demonstration, leaving their seats with 15 minutes left of the 1-1 draw against Arsenal in March 1978 (above); supporters wait patiently for tickets outside St Andrew's in February 1975 (below)

The new stand is opened in September 1985, from left to right: Graham Hayles (manager of Remploy Factory, Birmingham), Don MacLean (local personality), Dr. Charles Pocock (External PR Manager for Remploy) and chairman Keith Coombes (above, left); St Andrew's stewards learn how to use fire extinguishers (above); the Railway End being prepared to accept 1,500 seats in time for the new season (left); head groundsman Geoff Warren shows off the new sprinkler system, new seating and the new executive boxes in the Main Stand (opposite)

Young supporters help clear the St Andrew's terraces of snow in 1986 (above); Tessa Goulding takes a break from cleaning the executive boxes at St Andrew's (left); a message for the Midlands from one young fan at snowy Birmingham City (opposite, top); a Danish influence reaches the heart of the Midlands in 1981 (opposite, below)

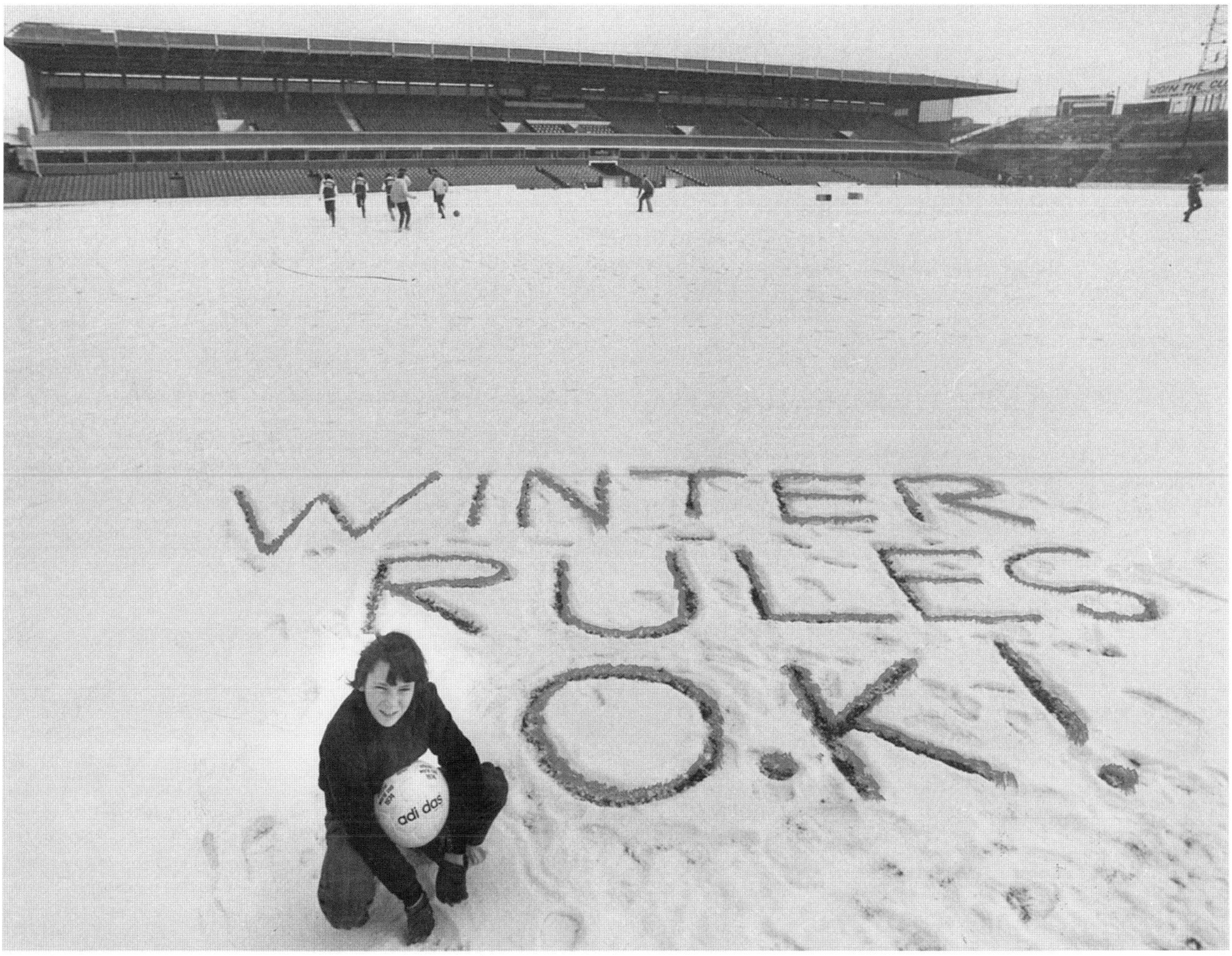
WINTER
RULES
O.K!
adi das

Näkki Nøkken

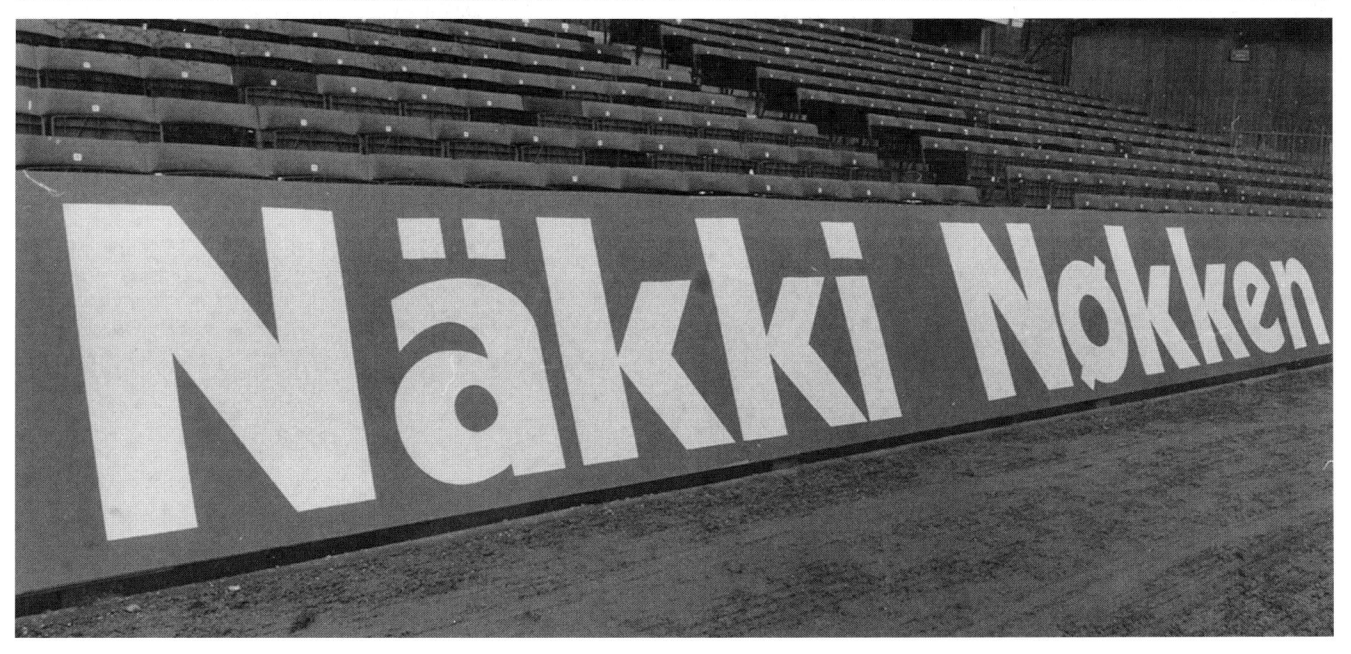

Birmingham City's Clean Up Campaign receives a welcome response in March 1982

Aerial shot of St Andrew's and the surrounding area (above); police form a line on the pitch in a bid to prevent disruption at the notorious Birmingham City v Leeds United match in May, 1985 (left)

Newly installed high fencing at the Tilton Road End, 1980s

West Ham United supporters are housed behind the new anti-riot fencing at St Andrew's for the opening game of the 1985/86 season (left)

The view of the pitch at St Andrew's from the police box during the match against Leyton Orient, September 1990 (opposite page, top) while police officers scan the crowd for any disturbances at the same game (right)

A copy image of the artwork for the proposed new stadium development, December 1993 (left); supporters prepare to enter the stadium ahead of the Nationwide Division One clash with Norwich City, January 2000 (below)

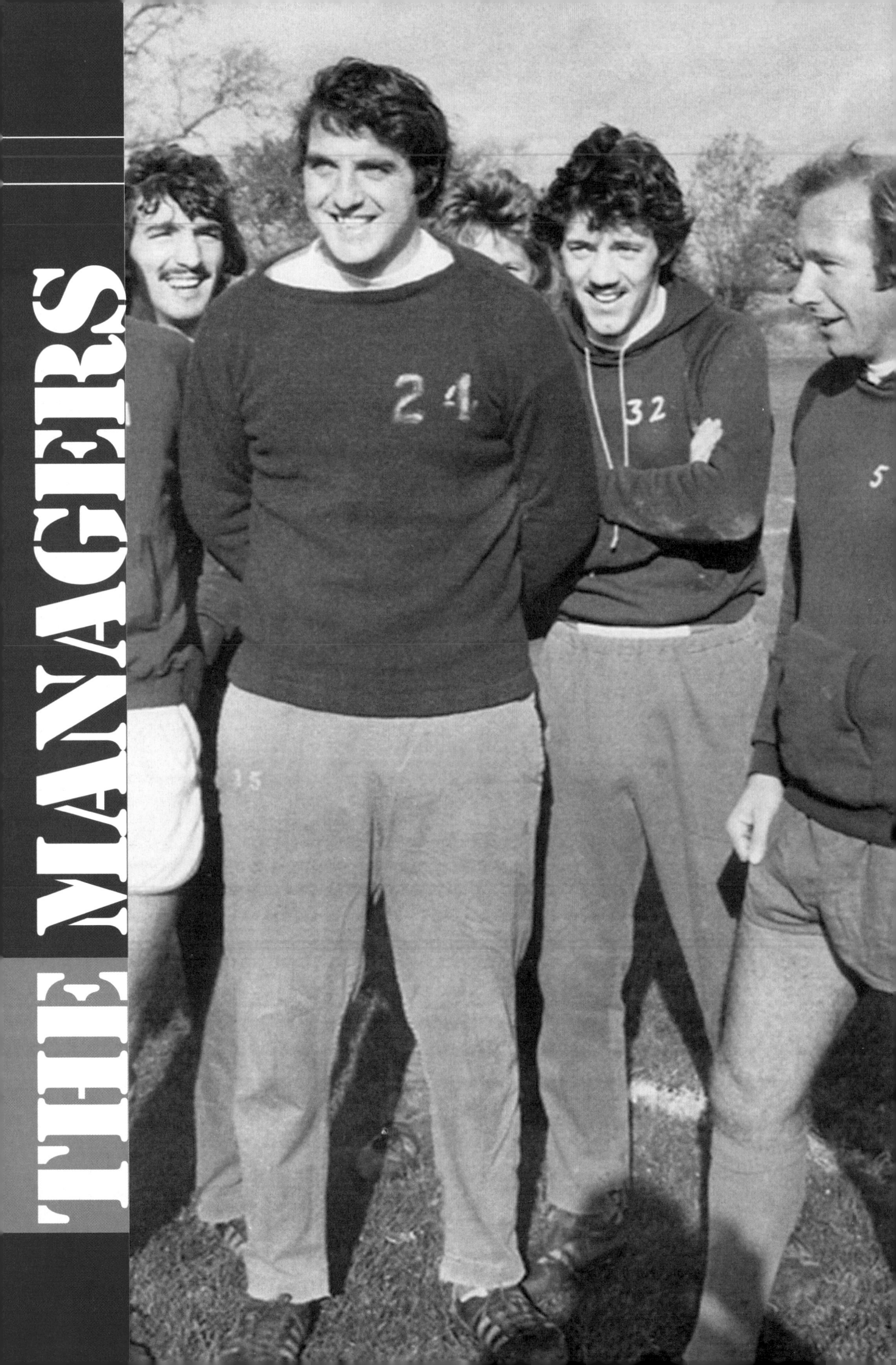

FROM first manager Bob McRoberts to Steve Bruce, taking in Merrick, Cullis, Ramsey and the rest. Here are the bosses you loved and the ones you loved to see go. Here's a complete analysis of the 27 men who have held the top job at St Andrew's . . .

No.1 Bob McRoberts (1910-15)

Birmingham City's first manager brought about instant improvement

McRoberts, who had been a distinguished player for the club during the Muntz Street days, was the first "official" manager of the club. Prior to that, the team was selected by a committee, usually headed up by the trainer or the secretary.

As the name suggests, McRoberts was a Scotsman and his appointment did much to aid the club at a time when times were hard at St Andrew's. Birmingham had finished at the bottom of the Second Division just before his arrival and so, in one sense, he could hardly make matters worse. McRoberts appointed Bill George, the former England international goalkeeper, as his trainer and there was an instant improvement in player professionalism. Under McRoberts, Birmingham pushed for promotion to the First Division but the squad never quite had the necessary class to finish in the top two. Soon after the First World War began in 1914, McRoberts decided to resign.

No.2 Frank Richards (1915-23)

In the wake of the First World War, promotion to the top flight

After the departure of Bob McRoberts, Birmingham were in no hurry to appoint an official replacement.

The club seemed happy for Frank Richards, the club secretary, to head up a committee that selected the team. This was not a problem in 1915 because competition football was put on hold because of the First World War but it was a risk when the Football League re-opened in 1919.

Surprising, then, that Birmingham should win the Second Division championship under Richards in 1921. In the First Division, Birmingham then finished in 18th position, then 17th, before Richards decided to relieve himself of selection duties in May 1923.

Richards was an interesting character. In 1920, presumably overburdened by the stresses of club management, he forgot to enter Birmingham for the FA Cup. It was an oversight that was unthinkable even then. "It was just one of those things," Richards said.

No.3 William Beer (1923-27)

Former player who signed the great Harry Hibbs

Beer was a player for the club from 1901-10. He was there for the name-change from Small Heath to Birmingham, and for the move from Muntz Street to St Andrew's. Then he went to Australia to run his own farm before he returned, very properly, to run a pub next to Villa Park. With his surname, there could have been no more appropriate position. But Beer missed football and it was no surprise when Frank Richards, the Birmingham secretary,

offered him the job as team manager. Beer agreed, so long as he could continue serving beer at his own pub.

Beer did not seem to enjoy being the manager of Birmingham. He seemed depressed that players of the Twenties seemed to lack the enthusiasm of his own era. The Birmingham directors wanted Beer to stay, despite indifferent results, but he was no longer convinced that he was the right man for the job. Beer's most famous decision was to sign Harry Hibbs, the goalkeeper, who would go on to become one of the best in the club's history and also an England international. Beer gave total commitment to his pub and he would often attend Birmingham's matches at St Andrew's, as a fan.

No.4 Leslie Knighton (1928-33)

Tactics are introduced - and a first Wembley appearance

After Frank Richards enjoyed a spell as caretaker-manager, Knighton took the job at the Annual General Meeting in the summer of 1928. Knighton was so quiet, it was hard to tell if he was in the room. But he was a friendly man and perhaps the first manager of Birmingham to vary team tactics according to the players available.

Knighton had been an undistinguished player but, after being forced to stop because of an ankle injury, he learnt the coaching side of the game. He was a good student. In May 1919, he took over as the secretary-manager of Arsenal, before assuming a similar but more liberating

Alex James - Leslie Knighton came close to signing him for Blues

1920-32 with Birmingham, making 345 appearances. Alas, he was not as effective as a manager. Birmingham employed a fine squad of players but Liddell was unable to build on the fine work of Leslie Knighton.

Under Liddell's watch, Birmingham were relegated to the Second Division in 1939, after 18 successive years in the top flight. These were difficult days at St Andrew's, especially with war clouds hovering menacingly over the British Isles. Liddell resigned from football during the War, took up teaching, and eventually became the headmaster at Handsworth Secondary Modern Boys School.

No.6 William Camkin (1939-45)

Man who helped keep the club alive during the Second World War

Even when the German bombs were turning St Andrew's into a wreck, Camkin was keeping the club alive.

Although he was officially selecting the team during the wartime matches, he was in effect aided by George Blackburn, who coached and trained the team.

Camkin was also the managing director of Birmingham and his presence during the Second World War was as significant as that of Harold Morris at the turn of the century.

Football clubs need men of such stature but they did not have Camkin for long. He resigned as a director because of ill health in 1953.

position in 1925 with Bournemouth, then of the Third Division South. Birmingham noticed his work and made an approach. The lure of the First Division was too tempting for Knighton and he accepted the job at St Andrew's.

Knighton tried to sign Alex James from Arsenal but was unsuccessful. He came closer to winning the FA Cup when he led Birmingham to the final at Wembley in 1931, but West Bromwich Albion, then of the Second Division, won 2-1.

Knighton left Birmingham at the end of the 1932-33 season to take over as the manager of Chelsea. He remained in London until the outbreak of the Second World War and later took over as the manager of Shrewsbury Town.

He retired in 1941, moved to Bournemouth, and became secretary of a local golf club. He died, aged 75, in May 1959.

No.5 George Liddell (1933-39)

Former player who was unable to build on previous success

George Liddell was one of those players who, like Steve Bruce in later years, was always planning for the day when he would eventually become a manager.

Liddell had been a fine player from

He supported the club until his death and would have been proud of his son, John, who later became a director with Coventry City.

No.7
Ted Goodier (1944-45)
A brief stint at the club now known as Birmingham City

For a six-month interlude during the War, Goodier took over as the manager of Birmingham, who were now known as Birmingham City. A Lancastrian, Goodier played for Huddersfield Town, Oldham Athletic and Queens Park Rangers before taking over as the player-manager of Rochdale in August 1939.

This was not a good time to start a new job - the Second World War was but a few days away - but Goodier was a loyal man and he remained in charge at Spotland until 1952. Rochdale were happy to let Goodier spend time with Birmingham, although the arrangement was only ever temporary. Goodier later managed Wigan Athletic and Oldham and died in 1973.

No.8
Harry Storer (1945-48)
All-rounder who delivered success to Blues

Storer was of the old school. Discipline was everything for a man whose father, Harold, was a goalkeeper for Arsenal and Liverpool and a cricketer for Derbyshire. Storer was born in Liverpool and played as a wing-half for Grimsby Town and Derby County, before appearing twice at full international level for England. He later played for Burnley and then took over as the manager of Coventry City, leading the club to promotion from the Third Division South in 1936.

Storer was the best Birmingham manager since Leslie Knighton. He led the club to the FA Cup semi-finals and the Football League South wartime championship in 1946 after only one season in charge. In 1948, creating the most disciplined Birmingham defence to date, the club won the Second Division championship. This should have been the start of serious success at St Andrew's but Storer returned to Coventry in November 1948, remaining at Highfield Road until 1953. Storer later took over as the manager of Derby County. He died, aged 69, in September 1967.

No.9
Bob Brocklebank (1949-54)
Built the foundations for future triumphs

Brocklebank could count, among his former clubs, Aston Villa and Burnley. He cut his managerial teeth with Chesterfield in 1945 before he joined Birmingham in January 1949. Brocklebank steadied Birmingham after the surprise departure of Storer and led the club to the FA Cup semi-finals in 1951. It was Brocklebank who signed Eddie Brown, Alex Govan and Jeff Hall, building the foundations for what would become the finest Birmingham team of the 20th century. But he would not reap the benefits. He left in October 1954, took over as manager of Hull City in 1955, and then Bradford City in 1961. He died in September 1981.

No.10
Arthur Turner (1954-58)
Delivered promotion and a cup final appearance

Turner spent nine years with Birmingham as a player but, because of the Second World War, missed out on the finest years of his career. He more than made up for that in four years as the Birmingham manager.

He was easily the club's most successful manager of the 20th century and, perhaps, the best to be employed at St Andrew's in 100 years.

In some ways Turner was fortunate. The tide was already turning in Birmingham's favour towards the end of the Bob Brocklebank era. Turner's predecessor had signed some talented players and Birmingham were swiftly on the rise, gaining promotion from the Second Division in 1955 and reaching the FA Cup final in 1956. This was Birmingham's golden period and Turner's role will never be forgotten.

He had been a solid defender with Stoke City before the Second World War and he spent much of his career playing alongside Stanley Matthews. He won a Second Division championship medal in 1933 and, just before the War, joined Birmingham.

He later played for Southport then took over as the manager of Crewe Alexandra. He returned to St Andrew's after a spell as the assistant manager of Stoke and he built on the foundations laid by Brocklebank. This was a good time to be a Birmingham supporter.

But Turner's departure, in September 1958, was as surprising as that of Brocklebank.

Pat Beasley, pictured at St Andrew's during his time as sole manager of City

He took over as manager of Oxford United, signed a youthful Ron Atkinson, and steered the club from non-League football into the Second Division. He later acted as a scout for Sheffield Wednesday and died in the mid-Eighties.

No. 11

Pat Beasley (1958-60)
Joint manager, then guided the club to first European final

Beasley (real name Albert Beasley) won a League Championship medal with Arsenal in 1934 but missed out on two FA Cup finals with the club. He joined Huddersfield Town in 1936 and picked up an FA Cup runners-up medal in 1938. The War cut short his career, but not before he won one England cap in 1939. He was a fine winger for Fulham after the War and moved to Bristol City as player-manager in 1950.

He remained in Bristol until February 1958 when he was offered the chance to move to St Andrew's. Initially, Beasley misunderstood the offer. He assumed he was joining Birmingham to become assistant to Arthur Turner. This was not the case. In fact, Harry Morris junior, the Birmingham chairman, wanted Beasley to work alongside Turner as a joint manager.

This arrangement became official in February 1958 but it did not work out. Turner resigned in September 1958 and Beasley became the acting manager before assuming the role on an official basis in January 1959. Under Beasley, Birmingham reached the final of the European Inter-cities Fairs Cup in 1960. He resigned in May 1960, took over as manager of Dover for four years, before seeing out his days in Somerset. He died in February 1986.

No. 12

Gil Merrick (1960-64)
Blues' goalkeeping legend - opened with a European final, and clinched first major prize

Merrick spent nearly a quarter of a century at St Andrew's and is, rightly, regarded as one of the most significant men in the history of the club.

When the club's records are published a century from now, there will be a special place for this fine goalkeeper and equally fine manager.

When he retired from a playing career that stretched from 1939-60, he was offered the chance to take over from Pat Beasley.

Merrick is surely the first manager to open up with a European final. When he took over at St Andrew's, his first task was to prepare the team for the European Inter-cities Fairs Cup final, second leg away to Barcelona. It was an arrangement that would seem unthinkable now, but then, Merrick had grown used to the demands of Continental football. He had, after all, been the England goalkeeper in the Fifties.

Birmingham lost to Barcelona but Merrick saw opportunities to learn. He spent much of the summer of 1960 conducting a study of Spanish football. In some ways, he was ahead of his time. In others, he seemed too serious for the early Sixties when British culture was changing dramatically.

He led Birmingham to the Fairs Cup final again in 1962. This time they lost to AS Roma of Italy. This was not a sign that Birmingham were in decline

Blues goalkeeping legend Gil Merrick tests out the St Andrew's surface

but the league positions were. Birmingham were usually involved in fights against relegation and Merrick could not stem the tide.

Success in the 1963 League Cup final (a two-legged affair against Aston Villa) merely papered over the cracks.

He survived in the job until June 1964, took over as the manager of Bromsgrove Rovers, then Atherstone Town, before becoming a personnel officer.

No. 13

Joe Mallett (1964-65)
Unable to halt decline into Division Two

Mallett replaced Gil Merrick, initially as caretaker-manager, before taking the position on a permanent basis. He made his name as a reliable defender with Southampton before taking a position as a coach with Nottingham Forest in 1953. The times were not kind to Mallett. Birmingham were in decline, players were expressing a desire to leave St Andrew's and the team were relegated in 1965. He was handed a new contract in May 1965 but the increased stability did not help him, his club or his team. In December 1965 he agreed to step down and he was happy to work alongside Stan Cullis, the new manager, as a coach. Mallett remained at St Andrew's until March 1970, after which he worked in Greece and with Southampton.

No. 14

Stan Cullis (1965-70)
Legendary manager unable to match Molineux feats

Coincidentally, or otherwise, the arrival of Stan Cullis seemed to usher in a period of stability. The former Wolverhampton Wanderers and England defender was among the most respected players of his era. He won an FA Cup runners-up medal in 1939 but was more successful as a manager. With Wolves, he won the FA Cup twice and the League Championship three times. He is easily the best manager in their history. Cullis left Wolves acrimoniously in 1964, turned down a job with Juventus and vowed never to return to football. A surprise, then, that he soon turned up at St Andrew's.

Cullis did not come close to achieving similar feats during his time at St Andrew's but that was not necessarily his fault. Birmingham became a strong cup team - they reached the FA Cup semi-final and the League Cup semi-final under Cullis - but consistency was lacking in the league. Cullis could not take Birmingham into the top flight. In many ways, however, he laid the foundations for the squad that would eventually lead Birmingham back into the First Division in 1972.

Cullis was a master tactician, a good man-manager, but Birmingham spent all of the Sixties in transition, without any clear direction. Had Cullis taken over in the late Fifties or early Seventies, things might have been different. But the late Sixties were strange times. Perhaps Cullis's greatest contribution at St Andrew's was signing Garry Pendrey and Bob Latchford.

Cullis later became a travel agent and died in February 2001.

Stan Cullis - Unable to recreate Wolves' success at St Andrew's

No. 15

Fred Goodwin (1970-75)
Shrewd signings pave the way for promotion success

Fred Goodwin was the right man at the right time. He put together a fine squad of players at St Andrew's and, deservedly, reaped the benefits.

It was Goodwin who signed Alan Campbell and Gordon Taylor; it was Goodwin who led Birmingham to promotion from the Second Division in 1972, the FA Cup semi-finals in 1973 and 1975, and generally made the team more attractive. Goodwin also gave a debut to Trevor Francis.

This was no surprise. Goodwin had been one of the original 'Busby Babes'. He played for Manchester United in the 1958 FA Cup final and appeared more than 100 times for the club.

He later played for Leeds United, managed the New York Generals in the North American Soccer League and then took charge of Brighton & Hove Albion. To prove his versatility, he also played cricket for Lancashire.

Just as Birmingham seemed set for success, their fortunes took a turn for the worse.

In September 1975, a few months after Birmingham reached the FA Cup semi-finals, Goodwin lost his job.

Whatever the frustrations, however, his period at St Andrew's is rightly regarded with affection, for his Birmingham teams were so good to watch.

Fred Goodwin (centre) surrounded by (from left to right) Howard Kendall, Trevor Francis, Kenny Burns and Joe Gallagher

No. 16

Willie Bell (1975-77)
Former Leeds defender fails to improve on Goodwin era

Willie Bell was born in Scotland and he made his name as a player with Leeds United in the Sixties, playing in the 1965 FA Cup final and picking up a runners-up medal.

Bell also played twice for Scotland, including a match against Brazil. When Bell replaced Goodwin, the change in atmosphere was dramatic.

Bell was calm, composed, collected and not given to displays of great emotion.

His problem was that he could not improve upon the work done by Goodwin. Birmingham lost their first five matches of the 1977-78 season, despite a number of new signings, and his position was untenable.

Bell then replaced Graham Taylor as the manager of Lincoln City and, at the start of 1979, moved to Virginia, USA, to join a religious cult and coach football.

No. 17

Alf Ramsey (1977-78)
England's World Cup-winning boss moves from boardroom

Offering the position to Alf Ramsey was no publicity stunt.

The manager of England when they won the World Cup in 1966, Ramsey was already on the board of directors at St Andrew's. Appointing him as Bell's replacement seemed appropriate.

Ramsey was a good player - he made his name as a full-back with Tottenham Hotspur - and a brilliant manager. He led Ipswich Town, then an unfashionable club, to the League Championship in 1962 and his success with England was, of course, unprecedented.

He lost his job with England after failing to lead the national team to the 1974 World Cup.

He joined the Birmingham board in January 1976 and provided much wisdom at a time when the club seemed set for serious success.

But Ramsey did not seem to enjoy the job. When Birmingham lost five and drew two of seven matches in November and December 1977, he cut a disillusioned figure. He resigned in March 1978, ostensibly through ill health.

Of all the official managers at St Andrew's (excluding caretaker-managers), the reign of Ramsey was the shortest in the club's history.

He retired, moved back to Ipswich, and died in 1993, aged 79.

His loss was mourned throughout the world.

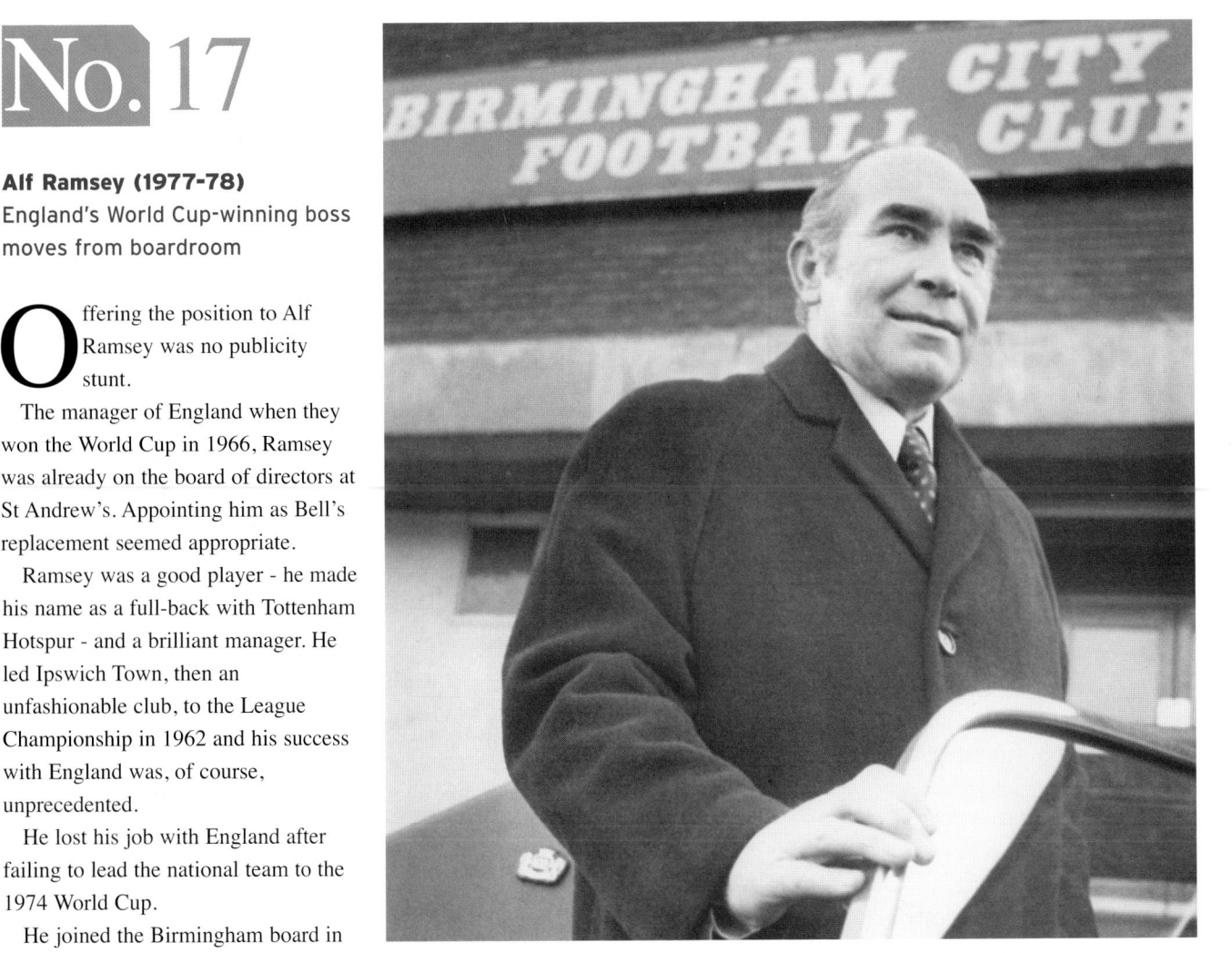

England to St Andrew's: Alf Ramsey did not seem to enjoy his stint as manager

No. 18

Jim Smith (1978-82)
Rollercoaster ride with the man known as the Bald Eagle

Jim Smith was one of those men who always looked old. It did not help that he was bald from an early age. He was nicknamed the 'Bald Eagle' long before he was famous. He was born in Sheffield in 1940 and spent his playing career with such lower-ranking clubs as Aldershot, Halifax Town, Lincoln City, Boston United and Carlisle United. It was while with Boston that he acquired a taste for coaching, for it was there that he accepted a position as player-coach. He then took over as the manager of Colchester United in 1972 and Blackburn Rovers in 1975. His appointment at St Andrew's was seen as an encouraging sign.

But his time with Birmingham was erratic. He took the club down in 1979, secured promotion in 1980 and created the talented team of 1981. Smith signed Alan Curbishley, Archie Gemmill, Colin Todd, Frank Worthington, Don

69

Givens and Willie Johnston and the football at St Andrew's was always good to watch. Smith was not averse to a gamble. Just after Argentina won the World Cup in 1978, Smith signed one of their defenders, Alberto Tarantini, who proved to be talented but capricious and, ultimately, unsuccessful. Tarantini did not last the season and Birmingham failed miserably in 1978-79.

By February 1982, Birmingham were not producing the results expected of such a talented squad. Smith was asked to resign and his contract was terminated.

However, he is one of the few Birmingham managers to have done better after his stint at St Andrew's. Smith led Oxford United to a League Cup triumph in 1986, endured a spell with Newcastle United and he has provided stability with Derby County.

Unfortunately, on his return to Oxford as boss in March 2006 he was unable to prevent them from dropping out of the Football League.

One of the game's true characters, Smith became the first man to visit all 92 League grounds - as of 1986 - as a manager.

Jim Smith meets Trevor Francis (right)

No. 19

Ron Saunders (1982-86)
Mixed period for man who swapped Villa Park for Blues

Ron Saunders made his name by winning the League Championship as manager of Aston Villa in 1981.

He left in February 1982 to take over Birmingham City.

Three months later, Villa won the European Cup. Saunders spent four years with Birmingham although his strict discipline did not provide the club with success.

These were bleak years for the club. Birmingham were relegated in 1984, promoted in 1985 and doing poorly when Saunders left St Andrew's in January 1986.

He left to manage West Bromwich Albion.

By the end of the season, both Birmingham and Albion were relegated, meaning ultimately that Saunders had contributed to the downfall of both clubs.

Saunders did not cause the Birmingham decline but he will be forever linked with it.

It was not his fault that a riot at St Andrew's in May 1985 caused the death of a boy and the match against Leeds United to be delayed in what were dark days.

He survived at The Hawthorns until September 1987 when he was sacked. He left football, seemingly for good, and now leads a private existence, refusing all offers to talk about the game.

No. 20

John Bond (1986-87)
Unable to halt slide into lower reaches of the Second Division

When Bond arrived as manager, Birmingham had lost 15 and drawn two of the previous 17 matches. Worst of all, they had lost to Altrincham, a non-League club, in the third round of the FA Cup. Attendances had slumped. These were the days when Birmingham was ceasing to be a major player in Midlands football. Bond could not stem the tide and Birmingham slipped ominously towards the lower regions of the Second Division.

Bond lost his job at the end of the 1986-87 season. The surprising thing was that he was a relatively successful manager with Manchester City at the start of the decade. As a player, he distinguished himself with West Ham United in the Sixties, winning the FA Cup in 1964 and representing the Football League Select XI. At St Andrew's, however, he is linked with a period of depression.

Ron Saunders, pictured at the pre-season photocall, 1985 (centre, top); John Bond pictured with Fred Davies (centre, bottom)

No.21

Garry Pendrey (1987-89)
Good servant who failed to stop slide into the third tier

The rot had set in before Pendrey took over as manager of Birmingham but he was the man who led the team into the Third Division for the first time. This was unfortunate.

He had been a good defender for the club, providing stability for 13 years. He could not do the same as a manager and, with the club struggling financially and attendances dwindling, St Andrew's was no longer an attractive place.

Birmingham avoided relegation in 1988 but finally slipped into the Third Division in April 1989.

For the first time since 1892, Birmingham were no longer full members of the Football League.

They were now associate members, destined to play against such teams as Chester City, Bury and Mansfield Town.

No.22

Dave Mackay (1989-91)
Failed to help the club climb out of Division Three

David Mackay, born in Edinburgh, Scotland in November 1934, represented his national team on 22 occasions. He tied with Tony Book of Manchester City for the Football Writers' Association's Footballer of the Year Award in 1969 and was a brilliant utility player.

Mackay played for Tottenham Hotspur and was a significant part of their Double-winning team of 1961, FA Cup-winning teams of 1962 and 1967 and European Cup Winners' Cup-winning team of 1963. In 1968 he was transferred to Derby County. In 1971 he was appointed player-manager of Swindon Town but left after just one season to take charge of Nottingham Forest. He remained at the City Ground until October 1973, when he returned to Derby County as manager, taking over from Brian Clough.

In his second season in charge of the Rams, he guided them to the League Championship but he resigned in 1976, taking over as manager of Walsall. He only lasted with the Saddlers until 1977 and remained out of the game for almost a decade until being appointed manager of Doncaster Rovers in 1987. Mackay's mission at St Andrew's was to take the club out of the Third Division but he was unsuccessful. He retired from football in 1991 and was made an inaugural inductee of the English Football Hall of Fame in 2002.

Garry Pendrey gets his point across on the training ground (below)

Lou Macari celebrates Blues' first-ever Wembley final success, courtesy of the Leyland DAF Cup in 1991 (above left); Terry Cooper signs on flanked by then chairman Samesh Kumar (above right)

No.23

Lou Macari (1991)
Brief stint saw Wembley glory - then swift departure

Macari took over midway through the 1990-91 season, led the club to the final of the Leyland DAF trophy at Wembley, but did not take the team out of the Third Division. Birmingham won at Wembley but Macari was not found to be celebrating with his players. Three weeks later, it became obvious why. He left the club to take over as manager of Stoke City.

He was an attacking midfield player for Manchester United in the Seventies and Eighties. He was bought from Celtic in 1973, turning down a move to Liverpool. He made 373 appearances for United, scored 97 goals and won the FA Cup in 1977. After leaving United in 1984, he managed Swindon Town, West Ham United, Stoke City (twice), Celtic and Huddersfield Town. He also worked as a consultant on the development of a computer game called Super League Manager.

His sons Michael and Paul have also played professionally with Stoke, when Lou was manager of the club. His youngest son, Jonathan committed suicide in 1999 after being released from his contract at Nottingham Forest.

No.24

Terry Cooper (1991-93)
Achieved promotion - but could not survive new era

Cooper was a distinguished right-back in the Sixties and Seventies with Leeds United and England. He played in the famous match between England and Brazil in the 1970 World Cup. In the summer of 1991, he replaced Lou Macari as manager and steered the club into the Second Division in 1992.

These were days of dramatic change at St Andrew's and Cooper was a good appointment.

It was during the Cooper period that David Gold, Ralph Gold and David Sullivan took over at St Andrew's, providing the club with financial stability for the first time since the Seventies.

But, while Birmingham survived in the new First Division - just - it was not enough to suggest that Cooper was a long-term appointment.

Cooper left at the start of the 1993-94 season, Barry Fry replaced him, but Birmingham were heading back towards the third tier of English football (now known as the Second Division, after the creation of the Premier League in 1992).

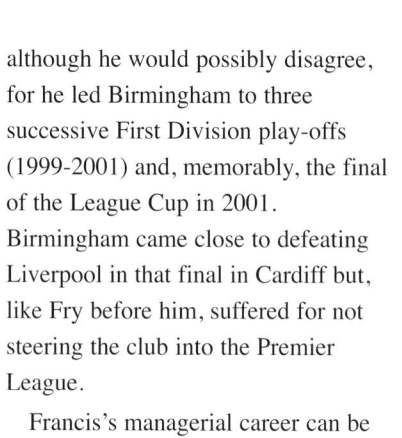

Barry Fry celebrates promotion at Huddersfield Town in 1995 (left)

No.25

Barry Fry (1993-96)
Never a dull moment as Blues look towards the top flight

In some respects, relegation seemed a blessing in disguise for Birmingham. They seemed to flourish for a time under Fry, even though the club's playing staff increased significantly. Birmingham ran Blackburn Rovers and Liverpool closely in the cup competitions but, most importantly, they gained promotion to the First Division. In December 1994, Birmingham smashed their record transfer fee paid by paying £800,000 for Ricky Otto from Southend United and then equalled this by buying Kevin Francis from Stockport County. Birmingham were crowned Second Division champions after defeating Huddersfield Town 2-1 with goals from Steve Claridge and Paul Tait. Fry also led Birmingham to success at Wembley in the final of the Auto Windscreen Shield.

But Birmingham craved Premier League football and Fry could not create a team good enough for promotion to the top flight. He left in 1996. St Andrew's was a quieter place without him.

No.26

Trevor Francis (1996-2001)
It's a case of so near, yet so far for City legend

Francis the Birmingham manager had nothing like the impact of Francis the Birmingham player, although he would possibly disagree, for he led Birmingham to three successive First Division play-offs (1999-2001) and, memorably, the final of the League Cup in 2001. Birmingham came close to defeating Liverpool in that final in Cardiff but, like Fry before him, suffered for not steering the club into the Premier League.

Francis's managerial career can be summed up by a succession of near-misses. He was always on the brink of success but never quite made it. It was the same with Sheffield Wednesday and Queens Park Rangers during the Nineties. But he was made for the job at St Andrew's.

Birmingham finished 10th in the First Division in his first season in 1997, and climbed to seventh the year after, missing out on the play-offs on goal difference. Then came the near-misses, the frustration, and, ultimately, the tears. He cried unashamedly after Birmingham lost to Liverpool on penalties in Cardiff and cut a frustrated figure when Birmingham lost to Preston on penalties in the 2001 play-off semi-final. He left in October 2001 and, two months later, turned up as boss at Crystal Palace. There was neat symmetry here. Francis replaced Steve Bruce at Selhurst Park just a few days after Bruce replaced Francis at City.

Trevor Francis leads Blues out in the 2001 League Cup final (above); Steve Bruce, pictured in summer, 2006 (above, right)

No. 27

Steve Bruce (2001-Present)
Premier dream fulfilled - now aiming to bounce back

Bruce appeared to have the midas touch when, within five months of taking over an underachieving squad of Birmingham players, he led the club into the Premier League after a memorable play-off final victory over Norwich

City in Cardiff. Probably no other manager could have achieved this for Birmingham. There is little doubt that Birmingham achieved their goal ahead of schedule, for few people expected such immediate success. But Bruce was determined to make the most of his capital.

He had been a successful defender for Manchester United, winning the Premier League title in 1993, 1994 and 1996, the FA Cup in 1990, 1994 and 1996, the League Cup in 1992 and the European Cup Winners' Cup in 1991.

At the end of the 1997-98 season, after a spell as a Birmingham player,

Bruce became player-manager of Sheffield United, a job which he held for just one season before beginning an 18-month spell as Huddersfield Town boss.

For the final two months of the 2000-01 season he was Wigan Athletic manager before being lured to Crystal Palace where he spent six months before being enticed back to Birmingham. These were the days when Bruce earned a reputation for lacking loyalty.

In 2002-03, Birmingham finished 13th in the Premiership and the following season climbed to 10th place in the final table. In 2004-05 they finished in 12th place.

In August 2004 Bruce was linked with the manager's job at Newcastle United - the club he had supported as a boy - but he turned it down. So much for lacking loyalty.

This was a decision that met with widespread approval among Birmingham supporters. Nobody could have predicted quite how badly the next two years would prove to be.

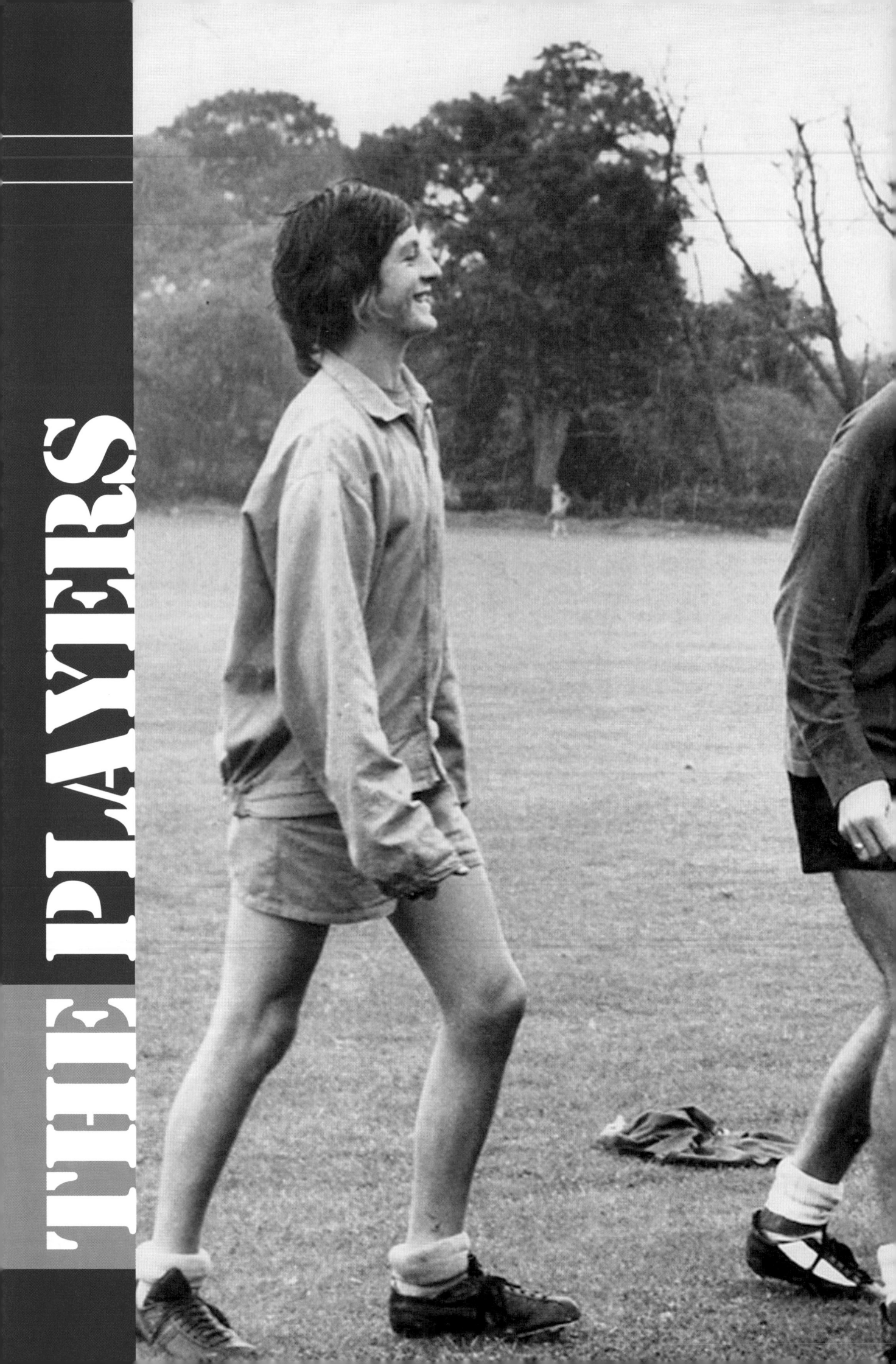

THE PLAYERS

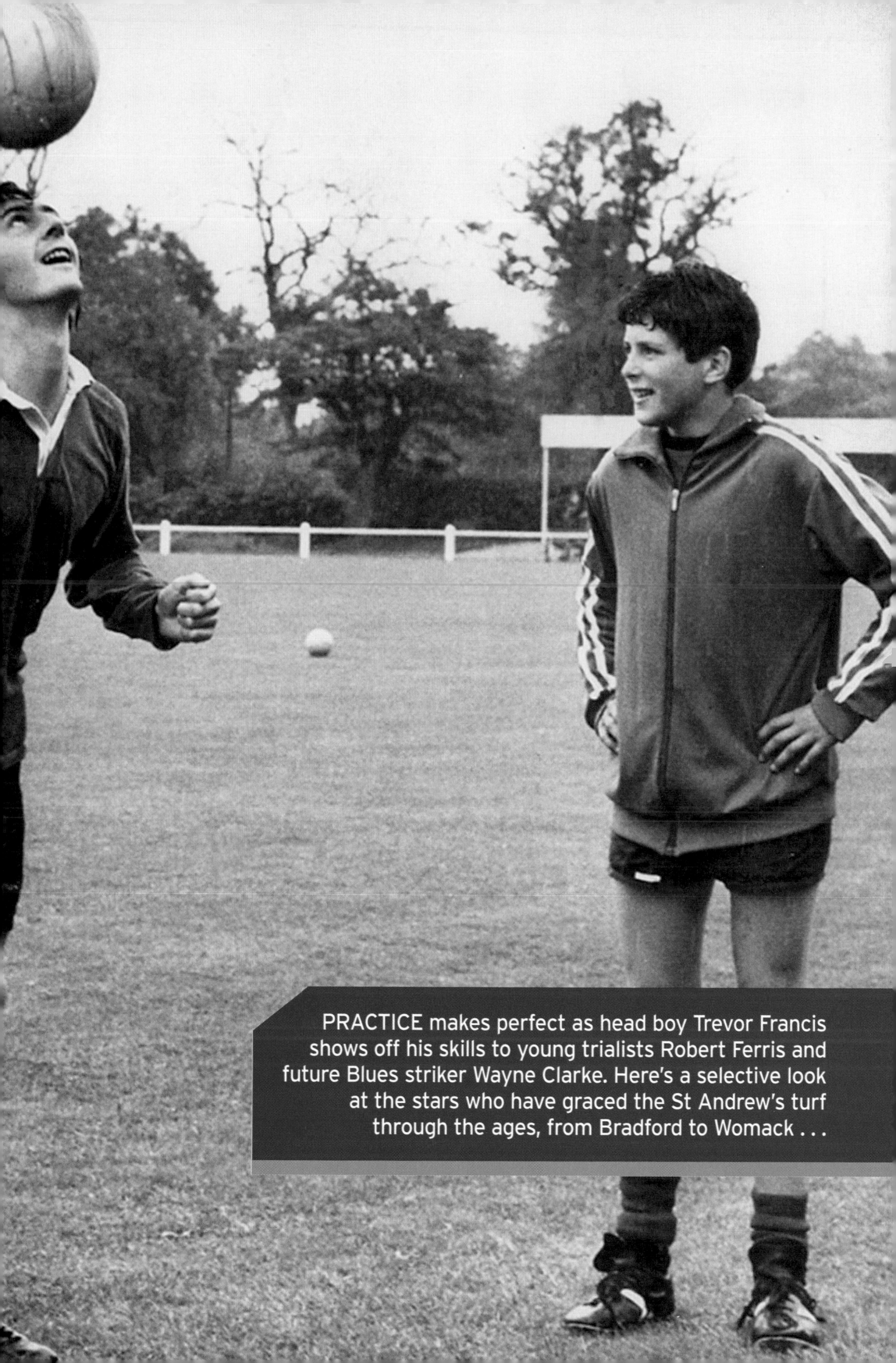

PRACTICE makes perfect as head boy Trevor Francis shows off his skills to young trialists Robert Ferris and future Blues striker Wayne Clarke. Here's a selective look at the stars who have graced the St Andrew's turf through the ages, from Bradford to Womack . . .

JOE BRADFORD (1920-1935)

Joe Bradford pictured left with chairman Keith Coombes (centre) and Bob Latchford (right) at a celebration to mark the club's centenary in 1975 (above); Joe on the run during his playing days (below)

He graced St Andrew's for 15 years and scored 267 goals in 445 appearances for Birmingham City, including Blues' goal in the 1931 FA Cup final (Birmingham lost to West Bromwich Albion).

They do not make players like Joe Bradford any more.

Like other players in Birmingham's long history, he had the misfortune of being around at the wrong time.

Had he flourished, for example, during the Trevor Francis era, he might have acquired the medals that his talent undoubtedly deserved.

It is easy to find Birmingham players with talent but less easy to find Birmingham players with winners' medals.

Bradford was similar to Dixie Dean, the Everton and England striker, and his contemporary, in being as adept in the air as on the floor.

Bradford's 32 goals during the 1927-28 season illustrated his class, while his decision to turn down Aston Villa to join Birmingham in 1920 - considered surprising at the time - said much about where his heart lay.

It was common in those days for players to remain with one club for their entire playing career.

The increased opportunities for travel in the Fifties and beyond made it easier for players to change clubs often during the course of their careers.

Now, it is rare for somebody to spend so long with one club.

With that in mind and with the changing nature of the game, it is unlikely that any player will break Bradford's Blues scoring record.

EDDIE BROWN (1954-1959)

With 90 goals in 185 appearances for Birmingham City, Brown was one of the pivotal figures for a team that reached the FA Cup final in 1956 and seemed on the brink of great achievements. He was a centre-forward of rare consistency, certainly a player who could have performed in any era. He also played in the team that won the Second Division championship in 1955, before taking his place at Wembley when Birmingham lost to Manchester City in the FA Cup final a year later. Not a bad track record for a man who wanted to become a priest.

Brown had character and humour. It is likely that he started the trend of wacky goal celebrations. Before the era of televised football, Brown would score and then shake hands with the corner flag. When talking to the media, he would quote passages of Shakespeare.

He was three-dimensional at a time when the media was only interested in a player's ability on the football pitch. In keeping with the nature of his varied interests, he retired from football to become a schoolteacher in Preston.

Top: Eddie Brown goes close for Birmingham City during the 1956 FA Cup final at Wembley; Eddie pictured fourth left at a club Christmas party (right)

ALAN CAMPBELL (1970-1976)

Birmingham City squad, pictured before the 1972/73 campaign. Campbell stands out with his distinctive look (below)

The Birmingham team of the mid-Seventies was easily the most attractive, if not necessarily the best, in the club's history.

This attractiveness had much to do with the presence of Alan Campbell, a long-haired Scot who looked like George Best and seemed to suit the era in which he played. The penguin shirt seemed to be made for Campbell, who oozed class at a time when football was made for television.

Campbell joined Birmingham from Charlton Athletic in 1970 and left for Cardiff City in 1976. In between, he worked well with Trevor Francis, and it remains a surprise that the team did not win anything during this period. He was part of the promotion team in 1972, when Birmingham finished as runners-up in the Second Division, but he was part of a squad that flattered to deceive. He played 202 matches for Birmingham, scoring only 14 goals from midfield, but did much to aid the development of Francis. When Campbell played well, Francis played well; when Francis played well, Birmingham played well.

KENNY CUNNINGHAM (2002-2006)

When he left Birmingham City on a free transfer in May 2006, Cunningham criticised everything about the club and its manager. This was out of character. During his four seasons with Birmingham, he was a talented, intelligent and articulate defender and one significant reason why the club was able to remain in the Premiership for four seasons.

Cunningham lacked pace but made up for that with a unique positional sense. He played in the 2002 World Cup for the Republic of Ireland and proved, even at the highest level, that brains can be as important as physical prowess. Cunningham never appeared out of control; never appeared flustered; never appeared out of his depth.

Towards the end of his Birmingham career, his body seemed to be giving up on him, but the mind was still working well. He perhaps spent a season too long at St Andrew's but Birmingham's defensive problems meant that he had little choice but to carry on. The season ended with relegation and Cunningham's time with the club ended shabbily.

Signed from Wimbledon in 2002, Cunningham forged a useful defensive partnership with Matthew Upson. Significantly, when these two players were injured, Birmingham stuttered. One was only able to fully appreciate Cunningham's importance to the team when he was out of it.

Kenny Cunningham leading City out against Wigan in 2006

CHRISTOPHE DUGARRY (2003-2004)

He only played 31 matches for Birmingham, and was only a full-time member of the staff for 10 months, but Christophe Dugarry had a profound effect on life at St Andrew's. Without him, Birmingham would surely have endured relegation in 2003.

His brand of skill, style and vision turned Birmingham from a workmanlike outfit into one that was pleasing to the eye. Well, what would one expect from a player who was in the France squad that won the World Cup in 1998.

Exquisite touches and dominance in the air were two of his many attributes. He lacked pace and rarely smiled, but he was talented enough to change the entire emphasis of Birmingham's play.

He was not the best player in Birmingham's history, simply because he was not there long enough, but he was certainly the most talented.

He was better for Birmingham when he was there on loan, from January-May 2003. After that, he seemed to lose interest and picked up a succession of niggly injuries.

His departure, in March 2004, was inevitable. He retired soon after and Birmingham's play reverted to a more simple, mundane style.

Dugarry fires a free-kick against Southampton (above); celebrating with Steve Bruce after scoring against Sunderland (left); thumbs-up after finding the target again, this time against Middlesbrough (opposite top, left); a job well done after victory at Charlton (opposite top, right); joining Stephen Clemence for an overhead kick against Chelsea (opposite, bottom)

phones
4u

Selsport

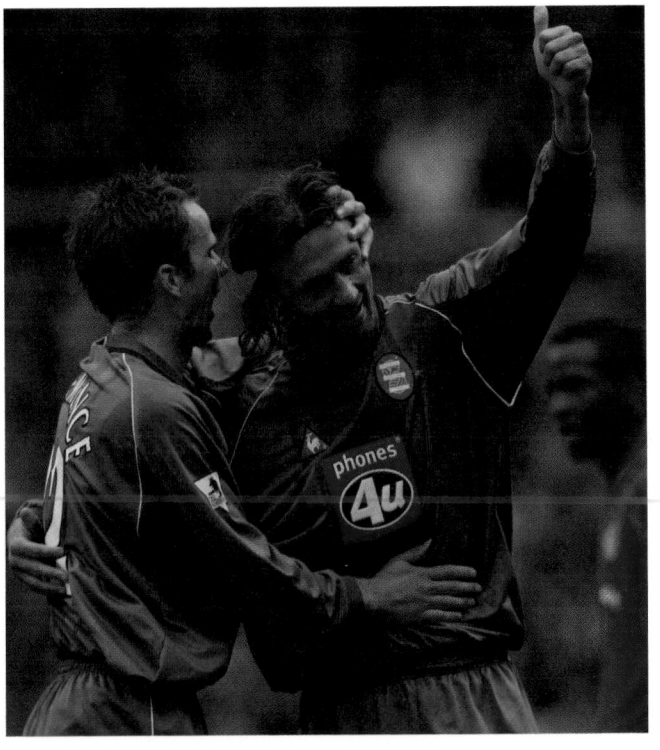

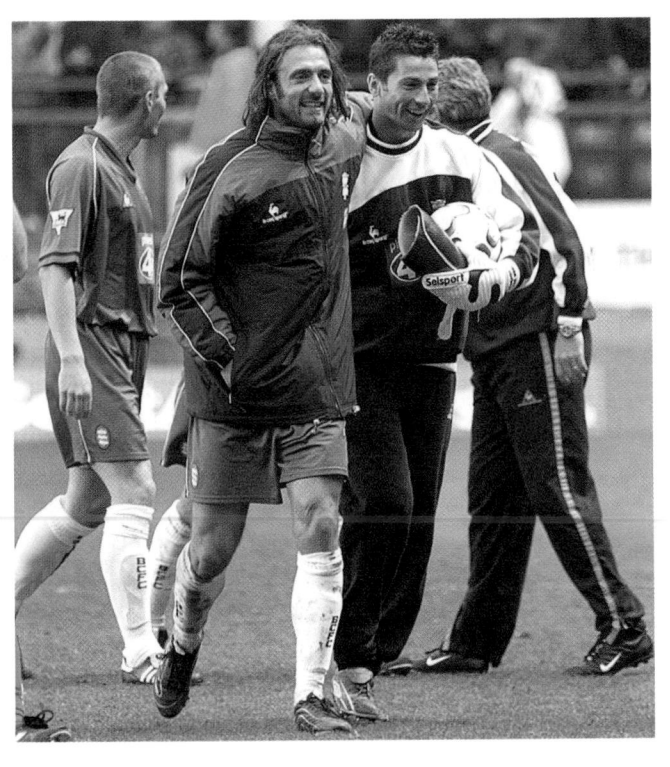

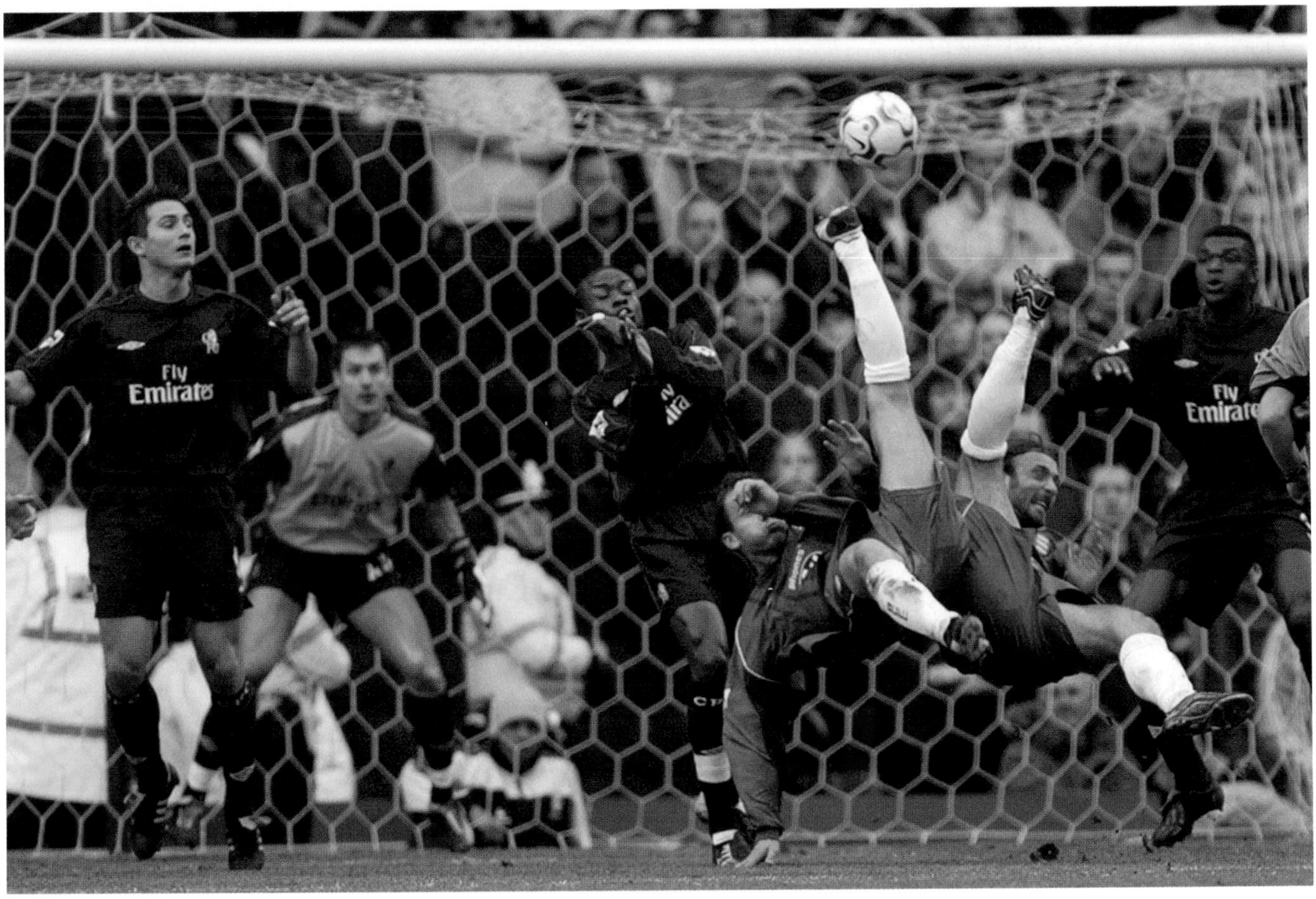
Fly
Emirates
Fly
Emirates

TREVOR FRANCIS (1970-1979)

Trevor Francis scored the winning goal for Nottingham Forest in the 1979 European Cup final, he played for England in the 1982 World Cup in Spain and made a lucrative move to Italy to play for Sampdoria. But he is inextricably linked with one club (Birmingham City) and one stadium (St Andrew's).

He burst onto the scene in 1970, aged 16, with a dubious hairstyle and a remarkable ability to keep control of the ball while running at speed. In the Seventies, when English football was in decline but was at its peak in terms of entertainment, Francis was the quickest player over the first five yards. It was that attribute that helped him to turn Birmingham City from an average Second Division team in 1971 into one that, by 1974, were among the most attractive in the top flight.

As has always been the case, the problem with having a good player - Francis scored 133 goals in 327 appearances for Birmingham and seemed to single-handedly keep them in the top flight - is that richer, more successful clubs try to sign him. This happened in February 1979 when Nottingham Forest, then the League title holders, signed him for £975,000.

The transfer was actually billed as the first for £1m in a publicity stunt that kept the supporters of both clubs happy. The deal effectively paid off for Forest just three months later when Francis scored with a diving header at the far post to secure the European Cup against FC Malmo of Sweden in the Olympiastadion, Munich. Francis remained at the top of his game for another five years but that was the greatest day of his career.

For a time, Francis was one of the most feared strikers in Europe, although he was part of an England team that underachieved badly. One might say that Birmingham underachieved while he was at St Andrew's. He was part of a forward line that included Bob Latchford, Kenny Burns and Bob Hatton. With players of that quality, Birmingham should have done better. Apart from an FA Cup semi-final place, Birmingham did not come close to winning a trophy

Trevor Francis on the run against Tottenham Hotspur at St Andrew's, March 1977

Trevor on target - 'his first televised goal' (above); mobbed having scored the vital second in the 2-1 win at Sheffield Wednesday in April, 1972 - promotion was near (below, left); on target in the 2-1 victory over Liverpool in August, 1976 (below, right)

in the Seventies.

But the lack of success does not detract from the memories inspired by Francis. In full flow, he was a delight to behold. Wearing Birmingham's penguin shirt in the early-to-mid Seventies, he was one of the pivotal figures of his time; a time when English football was magical. Years later, when Francis started to go bald, he became the manager of Birmingham and seemed to forget how to smile. He did a reasonable job, leading the team to the final of the League Cup in 2001 (they lost to Liverpool in a penalty shootout), but he could never lead the club to the Premiership. He suffered for that lack of success and, in November 2001, he resigned and went to his villa in Spain.

But Francis was a player first, manager second. It might even have felt wrong if his managerial achievements had eclipsed those of his playing days. He looked far better in a football kit than a managerial suit. He was probably at his peak when he played for England in the 1982 World Cup, where he scored twice - most notably against Kuwait in Bilbao - as the national team went to within two goals of a place in the semi-finals. England were unbeaten and should have done better but they suffered for their cautious attitude. Had midfielder Bryan Robson not picked up an injury during the tournament, and had the team played with more freedom, they would surely have reached the last four.

That would have given Francis a World Cup medal.

By the 1986 tournament, in Mexico, he was out of the international equation. Peter Beardsley and Gary Lineker had emerged as younger, faster and fitter alternatives. Francis was already seen as a link with English football's past.

Francis the man does not visit St Andrew's much these days but he remains ubiquitous. The Trevor Francis Suite at St Andrew's attracts thousands of visitors every season. The photographs of Francis that adorn the walls at St Andrew's are testimony to his prominent position in the club's heritage. The best player in Birmingham City's history? Absolutely.

On target (Trevor is grounded, second left) against Bristol City at St Andrew's in the Anglo-Scottish Cup in the late 1970s (above); Trevor cleaning boots in the changing rooms, circa 1970 (opposite page)

JOE GALLAGHER (1972-1981)

Joe Gallagher joins the forwards as Blues press for an equaliser against Leeds United

The Liverpool-born defender turned down Bill Shankly to sign for Birmingham City. Gallagher was seen as a player with the potential to replace Ron Yeats at Liverpool but Birmingham City offered greater opportunities for regular first-team football. And so it proved.

Gallagher joined Birmingham in 1972, remained at St Andrew's for nine years and played 335 matches for the club. Gallagher was part of arguably the most attractive Birmingham team in history - those of the 1973-76 era - but he made his mark as a centre-back who was rarely beaten in the air.

He won an international cap for representing the England 'B' team against Australia in 1980 but might have played for a full England team a couple of seasons earlier had it not been for a broken leg. He sustained the injury in a car crash in 1977, when he was at his peak, and he missed half of the 1977-78 season.

Gallagher signed for Wolverhampton Wanderers in 1981 for £350,000 although it is unlikely that Birmingham received all of the money. Wolves were suffering financial problems and their relationship with Birmingham was tarnished for a time. In the middle of this row was Gallagher, among the nicest guys to have played for Birmingham. After leaving Wolves, Gallagher played for West Ham United, Burnley and Halifax Town. He drifted into non-League football and was still playing in the North West Counties League in 1995. He still attends every Birmingham home match, in a journalistic capacity, and he looks the same as he did when he dominated the air in the First Division in the mid-Seventies.

JEFF HALL (1950-1959)

When he died of polio in 1959, aged just 29, the talented full-back should have been at his peak.

When he played for England in the mid-Fifties, the national team was briefly the best in the world. He was the right-back when England famously defeated Brazil 4-2 at Wembley in 1956. Hall, who also played in Birmingham's team that won the Second Division championship in 1955 and reached the FA Cup final a season later, appeared in all positions for Birmingham.

Centre-back was his most appropriate position. When his career ended, he had amassed 264 appearances for Birmingham in nine years from 1950. He represented England on 17 occasions.

When you played against him, you knew about it. He was tough and was rarely troubled by even the most talented of strikers. Even at international level, where the skill levels were more obvious, Hall remained in control.

After he died, the club constructed a scoreboard, with a prominent clock, and named it after him.

Jeff Hall in action during the 1956 FA Cup final (above, left); sampling the new gym equipment on offer at the club (above)

JIMMY HARRIS (1960-1964)

At a time when football was becoming more defensive, Jimmy Harris seemed to play as if it was still the early Fifties. His goalscoring ratio belonged to a more liberated era, rather than the constraints of the early Sixties. Although Harris made his name with Everton, he flourished with Birmingham, scoring 53 goals in 115 appearances from 1960-64.

With his curly hair, he resembled a latter-day Dixie Dean, but Harris was quicker, smarter, and more stylish. Harris was probably the fastest player to appear for Birmingham.

He is one of the few players in the club's history to have won a leading domestic honour, even if it was the League Cup, in the days when the tournament was shunned by the larger clubs.

It is to Harris's credit that, unlike most players of his era, he could strike the ball equally well with both of his feet. Nobody was sure if he was left-footed or right-footed, although it did not really matter because he probably did not even know.

This was a golden era for Birmingham and it might not have been so successful had Harris not been signed from Everton in 1960.

Jimmy pictured with the Blues squad, February 1961 (above - front row, third right). Top: In action (second from left)

BOB HATTON (1971-1976)

With 73 goals in 218 appearances for Birmingham City, Bob Hatton was clearly a master of his art. He played for the club at a time when Trevor Francis was making his mark and when Bob Latchford was developing into the player that would one day win England caps. Francis and Latchford took more of the compliments but Hatton did much of the hard work.

Hatton joined Birmingham from Carlisle United in 1971, left to join Blackpool in 1976, and made a significant impression in between. He was a versatile player, good in the air and he was a vital cog in the team that won promotion from the Second Division in 1972. Hatton played in all four divisions and seemed to be able to score from every angle. In all, he played 620 matches and scored 217 goals before retiring in 1983.

He did most of his best work on the left side of the forward line - some have likened him to Tony Hateley, his contemporary - and he was able to make full use of his impressive physique.

With such a strike-force, Birmingham should have done better in the mid-Seventies, but the memories are still sweet. Hatton later worked as a summariser on local radio.

Bob in action, top; Swindon Town defender Frank Burrows slides in to deny Bob at St Andrew's (right)

TERRY HIBBITT (1975-1978)

Hibbitt won a European Fairs Cup medal with Leeds United in 1968 but made his name with Newcastle United in the Seventies. He enjoyed two spells with Newcastle. Sandwiched in between, from 1975-78, was a distinguished spell with Birmingham City.

He revealed to St Andrew's regulars a sweet left foot and a quick brain. He was an impressive midfield player and, but for a succession of injuries, might have made the full England international squad. His only recognition at international level saw him make the England non-League team in 1986.

Hibbitt left Newcastle for Birmingham for £100,000. He played 122 matches for Birmingham, scoring 11 times (usually from set-pieces), before returning to Newcastle in May 1978.

Injuries forced Hibbitt to retire from professional football in 1980 but he was still a class act. He joined Gateshead, the Northern Premier League club, soon after and won a championship medal in 1983. He managed Gateshead in 1986 and, after leaving, ran a pub and a newsagent business in the North East.

Alas, he died of stomach cancer in August 1994. His brother Kenny was an equally talented player with Wolverhampton Wanderers in the Seventies.

Photo-call: Terry pictured during pre-season

Terry Hibbitt races away in delight after netting for Blues in the late 1970s

HARRY HIBBS (1924-1940)

There is much debate about who was the best goalkeeper in Birmingham City's history: Gil Merrick or Henry 'Harry' Hibbs. Hibbs made 389 appearances for the club during the inter-War years and was, in the period before there was a World Cup, the best goalkeeper in the world. He represented England on 25 occasions.

As a small and lightweight man, Hibbs looked far from ideal for a goalkeeper.

He made the first team in 1929 and remained first choice until the beginning of the Second World War.

Born in 1906 in Tamworth, he was part of a goalkeeping family that included uncle Hubert Pearson and cousin Harold Pearson, both of whom played for West Bromwich Albion.

Hibbs relied more on anticipation than agility but he was a clever goalkeeper.

He was the first footballer to be granted a wartime benefit match and then he became the manager of Walsall (1944-51). He ended his involvement in football as the manager of Welwyn Garden City in 1964.

He was probably at his peak when he toured South Africa with the England team in 1929. He was unfortunate. England were at odds with FIFA, the game's world governing body, and they did not enter the 1930 World Cup.

Hibbs certainly deserved a wider audience but he was content in the knowledge that he played in the 1931 FA Cup final, which Birmingham lost to West Bromwich Albion. He died in Hatfield, Hertfordshire in May 1984 four days before his 79th birthday, and the same month in which Birmingham endured relegation from the First Division.

Birmingham keeper Harry Hibbs dives as the ball whizzes past the post during a match in 1937

DAMIEN JOHNSON (2002-PRESENT)

There has never been a shrewder signing in Birmingham City's history. Johnson cost just £50,000 when he joined the club from Blackburn Rovers in March 2002. Small but perfectly formed, Johnson is the tough kid from Belfast who exemplified Birmingham's in-your-face style of play that scared the Premiership's most illustrious teams for two years.

Johnson is a versatile midfield player who seems to enjoy the physical dimensions of professional football. Unlike most men, Johnson seems to look better with a bloody nose and a bruised cheekbone. It belies his nature, for he is quiet, modest and unassuming.

He was brilliant for Birmingham during the 2005-06 season. Without him, Birmingham would have been relegated long before the end of April. A Northern Ireland international, he left Blackburn soon after winning a League Cup winners' medal with the Lancashire club. It was an odd decision to sell Johnson, but Birmingham were happy beneficiaries.

International: Damien Johnson in action in 2006 (right)

BOB LATCHFORD (1968-1974)

One has to wonder what type of anti-ageing cream Latchford uses. He looked younger in spring 2006, aged 55, than he did when he menaced defenders for Birmingham City in the early Seventies.

That is not the only mystery to surround Latchford. Equally intriguing is that he hails from a family that produced two professional goalkeepers. Dave Latchford was the Birmingham goalkeeper in the mid-Seventies; Peter Latchford was the West Bromwich Albion goalkeeper during the same decade.

Bob Latchford reached his peak from 1977-80 when, as the Everton striker, he was a regular in the England team and was as good in the air as he was on the ground.

For Birmingham, he scored 84 goals in 194 appearances, scoring 30 times during the 1971-72 promotion campaign.

Although he initially found it difficult to adapt to the pace of top-flight football, he soon forged a strong partnership with Phil Summerhill and Bob Hatton. Trevor Francis was also in the team at this time, so it was a surprise that Birmingham won nothing but friends.

The problem was that, while Latchford continued to improve, Birmingham did not. He asked for a transfer in February 1974 and joined Everton in a complicated deal that saw Howard Kendall move to Birmingham from Goodison Park, with Archie Styles also heading in the opposite direction.

Latchford later played for Swansea City, NAC Breda of the Netherlands, Coventry City, Lincoln City and Merthyr Tydfil, before retiring in 1986.

Bob acknowledges the applause of the crowd (left), while (above) Bob beats Ipswich Town captain Mick Mills to the ball during a cup tie at St Andrew's during the early 70s. Opposite page: Bob on the run, circa 1971

STAN LYNN (1961-1965)

Stan Lynn (right) with team-mate Colin Green, pictured before a game in 1963

The only player to have won leading honours with Birmingham City and Aston Villa, Stan Lynn was a significant figure in the city during the early-to-mid Sixties. He won a FA Cup winners' medal with Aston Villa in 1957, a League Cup winners' medal with Villa in 1961 and a League Cup winners' medal with Birmingham in 1963. He also won a Second Division championship medal with Villa in 1960.

The late Fifties and early Sixties were the golden period in the life of this fine man. There is little doubt that Lynn gave Villa the better years of his career but that was at a time when Villa had an abundance of good players. Given that Birmingham were in decline, it is fair to say that Lynn was more important at St Andrew's than he ever was at Villa Park. It is an interesting debate.

He left Villa to join Birmingham in 1961 and stayed until 1965, playing 148 matches and scoring 30 goals. It was rare in those days for a right-back to score so many goals and, remarkably, he was Birmingham's leading scorer in 1964-65. He once scored a hat-trick from his role in the back four.

He retired in 1968, was involved in a Villa all-stars team in the Seventies and played golf as often as possible. He died, aged 73, in April 2002 - just a month before Birmingham City reached the Premiership for the first time. He would have approved.

GIL MERRICK (1939-1960)

There is no doubt that Merrick is the best goalkeeper in Birmingham City's history. He could also claim, with some justification, as being one of the top-10 England goalkeepers in history. Merrick spent a quarter of a century with Birmingham, first as a player, then as a manager. He joined the club from Solihull Town in 1938, when Hitler still ruled Germany, and left as manager in 1964 when The Beatles were revolutionising the music industry. In between, he did rather better than Birmingham City.

He played 551 matches for the club - a record - and played in the 1954 World Cup for England. In some ways, he was unfortunate. Goalscoring was plentiful at the tournament in Switzerland and it was not a good time to be a goalkeeper. England lost 4-2 to Uruguay in the quarter-finals but they were still a decent team. By 1956, with Hungary and West Germany on the wane and Brazil still not at their peak, it is probably recognized that England were the best team in the world. But Merrick was no longer the England goalkeeper.

Alas, his international career will be defined by his two matches against Hungary. In 1953, he conceded six goals at Wembley; in 1954, he conceded seven in Budapest. In Hungary, they nicknamed Merrick 'Mister 13'. This is unfair, for Merrick flourished at a time when goalkeepers received little protection from referees or, indeed, the rules. Merrick was adept at handling the ball - most goalkeepers still preferred to punch the ball in those days - and he was remarkably athletic.

Just as his England career is notable for famous defeats, so, too, is his career with Birmingham. He was in goal when

Gil Merrick congratulates Manchester City goalkeeper Bert Trautmann (who, unbeknown to him at the time, had suffered a broken neck during the match) following City's 3-1 win in the 1956 FA Cup final

the club lost in the 1956 FA Cup final to Manchester City. That was the day, at Wembley, when Bert Trautmann broke his neck yet completed the match and ended up with a winners' medal.

Merrick kept his Errol Flynn moustache long after it was in fashion. He became the Birmingham manager in 1960 and, notably, led the club to its only significant honour - the League

Cup, in 1963. He was also in charge when the club reached the final of the Inter-cities Fairs Cup in 1961.

When he left the club, in June 1964, he still had the moustache and took with him enough memories to last a lifetime.

He was without doubt the best goalkeeper in the club's history and, probably, the best manager, too.

MALCOLM PAGE (1964-1981)

The fans invade the pitch as Blues book their place in the last 16 of the FA Cup - with Malcolm in the centre (above)

His career with Birmingham links the Gil Merrick era and the Jim Smith era. Page was loyal, quick and versatile. He represented Wales on 28 occasions and has played more international football than any other player in Birmingham's history.

Page was an expert at man-to-man marking. All those years of tackling at international level turned him into an adept full-back. He peaked during the mid-Seventies, when Birmingham were a joy to watch, and when success should have been just around the corner. At 5ft 9ins, he was not naturally suited to the central-defensive position but his height ensured that he was quick off the mark and a fierce tackler. Wingers hated playing against Page because, mentally, he was as quick as they were. He made 391 appearances for Birmingham, although he only scored 10 goals in that time. One of those goals was a memorable effort against Huddersfield Town in the FA Cup in 1972.

Malcolm Page leads the group in training at St Andrew's - trailing behind are (left to right) John Sleeuwenhoek, David Robinson and Mick Darrell

ROBBIE SAVAGE (2002-2005)

His popularity at St Andrew's deteriorated alarmingly in January 2005 when he initiated his own move to then Premiership rivals Blackburn Rovers. It was a dreadful act of disloyalty and one that still rankled over a year later. Savage, though endearing for a time, was a public-relations nightmare and his departure seemed to overshadow more important things at St Andrew's.

Savage arouses an extreme of emotions. You either like him or, more likely, dislike him. As a player, he made virtues of his vices to become an effective central midfield player. Some have said that he lacks skill and class but that criticism sticks because Savage is not really taken seriously. Actually, he passes the ball well, rarely gives it away, and has enough energy to maintain his high-tempo style for the entire 90 minutes.

One could argue that Birmingham's decline towards relegation from the Premiership began when Savage left. Steve Bruce never successfully replaced the player. Birmingham were never as good without Savage, proof, perhaps, that he was better and more effective than many believe him to be. Blackburn have certainly benefited since Savage moved there.

Savage played 88 matches for Birmingham until that crazy day, January 19, 2005, when he joined Blackburn for a mere £1.25m. As a team, Birmingham have not been the same since.

Robbie Savage striking a free-kick against Charlton in 2004 (above), and celebrating at Leeds a year previous (right)

TREVOR SMITH (1953-1964)

Trevor (left) backs up keeper Gil Merrick as Burnley No 9 Shackleton challenges in September 1959

When Trevor Smith played in the same Brierley Hill youth team as future 'Busby Babe' Duncan Edwards, there was a difference between the two. Smith was slight, Edwards was muscular.

Then the change occurred. Smith turned himself into a muscular player, a strong defender, who would go on to play twice for England and appear 430 times for Birmingham City.

Smith replaced Billy Wright in the England team at a time when Birmingham seemed on the brink of serious success. But, just as Birmingham could not fulfill their potential, so Smith failed to make the grade consistently at international level.

He made his Birmingham debut at the age of 17 and captained the team for a spell, impressing his team-mates with his consistency and strength. Towards the end of his Birmingham

career, he sustained a series of injuries but they were not enough to stop him from signing for Walsall in 1964.

Rumours were rife that Walsall were conned into signing an injured player because Smith seemed to lack the fortitude that made him so popular at St Andrew's.

After retiring from playing, he ran a pub in Tamworth and an off-licence in Birmingham city centre, before moving to Essex. Smith died in August 2003.

FRANK WOMACK (1908-1928)

Defender Trevor Smith (right) heads for goal against Everton at St Andrew's

Everything significant that happened to Womack seemed to come in a year ending in eight. He was born in 1888, joined Birmingham City in 1908, left Birmingham in 1928, and died in 1968. During 20 years with the club, he was the captain for 17 straight seasons and he played 515 matches - the longest-serving player in the club's history.

Interesting, then, that he is not famous for his loyalty, but for his role in a bribery scandal that failed miserably in 1913.

He was offered 55 guineas (£57.75) to fix the match between Birmingham and Grimsby Town. Womack, a bastion of integrity, reported the matter to the police and the football authorities and the culprit was arrested. Birmingham ended up losing the match 2-1.

Sadly, Womack left Birmingham under a cloud. He was 39 at the beginning of the 1928-29 season and the club decided that he was too old.

It was a shabby way to treat one of the club's all-time great players, and certainly the most loyal, and it rankled with him for years.

He won a Second Division championship medal in 1921 but, despite representing the Football League Select XI, he never won international caps for England.

He was given a trial for England but never convinced the selection committee – there was no England manager in those days - that he was of international standard.

He spent the final years of his career managing clubs like Grimsby Town, Leicester City, Notts County and Oldham Athletic.

He died in the same year that Bob Latchford signed professional forms for Birmingham City.

103

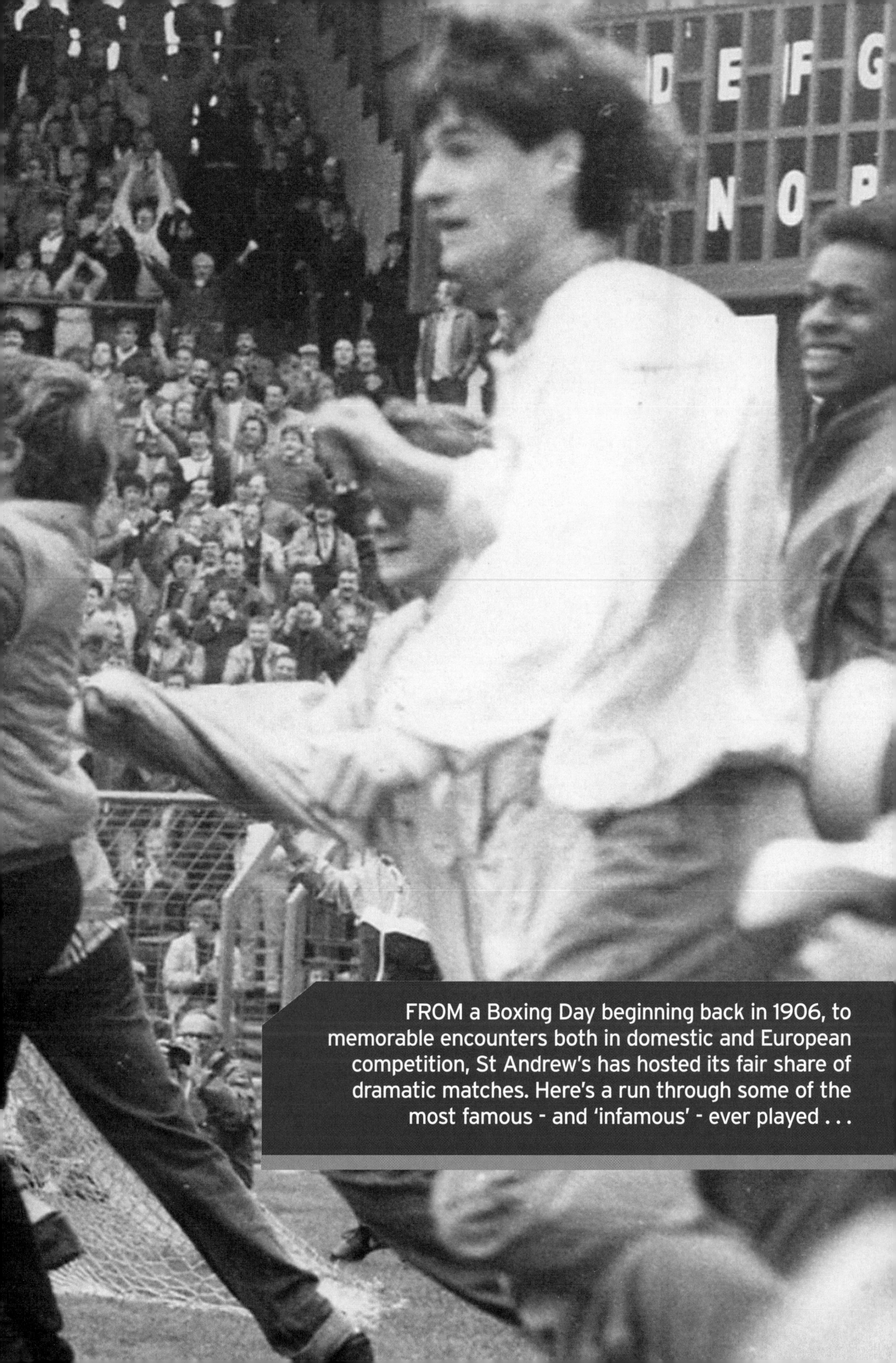

FROM a Boxing Day beginning back in 1906, to memorable encounters both in domestic and European competition, St Andrew's has hosted its fair share of dramatic matches. Here's a run through some of the most famous - and 'infamous' - ever played . . .

BIRMINGHAM 0
MIDDLESBROUGH 0
(DECEMBER 26, 1906)

For the first match at St Andrew's, Birmingham produced a special 'souvenir of the opening of the New Ground'. But there was a fear that few people would turn up, for snow turned the pitch into an expanse of white. The conditions were not conducive to good football and Birmingham were worried that their big day would be spoilt.

In the event, more than 32,000 attended the match, although the occasion was more memorable than the football. The goalless draw was inevitable - the brown ball would barely move on what looked like a bed of cotton wool - and the majority of supporters went home

Former ground at Muntz Street the season before the move to St Andrew's

frustrated.

But Birmingham would have been happy with the event. Their average attendance that season was a mere 15,315 - less than half the official crowd figure for that first match at St Andrew's.

BIRMINGHAM 8
NOTTINGHAM FOREST 0
(MARCH 10, 1920)

Birmingham were the great underachievers during the 1919-20 season. They were easily of First Division standard yet they spent a year longer in the Second Division than was necessary. Despite this memorable victory against Nottingham Forest, perhaps their most emphatic during the inter-War period, they finished third in the Second Division and failed to gain promotion.

With Harry Hampton and Joe Lane forming part of the forward line, Birmingham were always exciting to watch. Hampton was the player with flair and cunning; Lane the player with strength and fortitude. It was a partnership that worked well.

Forest were actually the better team until the latter stages of the first half. Birmingham were two goals ahead by then - Hampton scored both - but the most significant point of the match came just a few minutes before half-time when Hart, the Forest defender, broke a leg. Forest were down to 10 men - no substitutes in those days - and had little chance of keeping the score down.

The second-half rout, in front of more than 15,000 people, was inevitable. Lane scored the third with a first-time shot, Hampton scored the fourth (and his third) after Lane's shot hit the crossbar, and Lawrie Burkinshaw scored the fifth with a shot from 25 yards.

Burkinshaw scored the sixth after fine wing play by George Davies, Hampton scored the seventh after the Forest goalkeeper made a mistake, and Lane completed the scoring in the final minute.

Birmingham ended the season by picking up just three points from their final four matches to miss out on promotion. This was the first season after the First World War and City's average gate was 22,880.

BIRMINGHAM 2
EVERTON 2
(FEBRUARY 11, 1939)

St Andrew's was only 32 years old when it attracted its largest attendance.

A crowd of 67,341 was recorded for the FA Cup fifth-round tie against Everton in February 1939.

As St Andrew's moved towards its 100th birthday, the ground capacity was just over 30,000.

St Andrew's is certainly more comfortable now but was it ever as exciting as the day, just before the Second World War, when Everton came to town?

Unlikely.

Everton were one of the best teams in the world in 1939.

Birmingham were fighting against relegation to the Second Division.

The FA Cup provided relief for a Birmingham team that had lost its way. And yet, the two teams played out a surprising 2-2 draw.

Birmingham scored both of their goals against the run of play but they deserved their draw and a chance for a money-spinning replay at Goodison Park.

Owen Madden gave Birmingham the lead a minute before half-time, although his shot took a wicked deflection before it span away from Ted Sagar and into the goal. Everton equalised within 30 seconds through Alex Stevenson.

Wally Boyes, formerly of West Bromwich Albion, gave Everton the lead on the hour mark and Birmingham seemed destined for defeat.

But Madden headed home an equaliser in the 81st minute, and both teams could have scored a third goal that would surely have ensured victory.

Everton won the replay 2-1 but lost 2-1 to Wolverhampton Wanderers in the sixth round. They won the League Championship just as Birmingham endured relegation.

It was the last full league season until 1946-47. The Second World War came in September 1939 and St Andrew's would endure bomb damage.

By the end of the war, Birmingham had changed their name to Birmingham City and assumed a less provincial identity.

Birmingham - Division 2 champions, 1920-21

BIRMINGHAM CITY 9
LIVERPOOL 1
(DECEMBER 11, 1954)

Birmingham City were on the rise and heading for the Second Division title; Liverpool, pre-Bill Shankly, were in transition. There could be only one possible conclusion - a significant Birmingham victory.

This was a day when it all went right for Birmingham and the only surprise was that they did not surpass double figures. It is hard to say if Liverpool were dreadful because Birmingham were so good.

It has often been claimed that this Liverpool team lacked good players but that is not the case. They boasted Laurie Hughes, who had played in the 1950 World Cup as a defender for England, and Alan A'Court, who would play as a winger for England in the 1958 World Cup. And then there was Billy Liddell, one of the top-20 players in the club's history. On the day, however, it was Birmingham who boasted the class players.

Less than a minute had gone when Jackie Lane opened the scoring and Liverpool never recovered. Eddie Brown scored the second and third, before Liddell reduced the arrears with a fine goal on the break. Any hope of a Liverpool recovery ended when Gordon Astall scored Birmingham's fourth goal.

The second half was surreal; probably the best that Birmingham have enjoyed in 100 years at St Andrew's. They scored five goals and could have scored five more on top of that. It was that type of afternoon. Astall scored the fifth, Peter Murphy the sixth, Alex Govan the seventh, Murphy the eighth and Brown the ninth. Brown's performance in scoring a hat-trick was as good an individual display by any Birmingham player at St Andrew's.

That season Birmingham romped to the Second Division title. They drew 2-2 with Liverpool at Anfield the following April before ending their campaign with a 5-1 victory at home to Doncaster Rovers. Ten seasons later, Liverpool reached the semi-finals of the European Cup and won the FA Cup. Birmingham finished bottom of the First Division.

Blues team photo, circa 1956

BIRMINGHAM CITY 3
BORUSSIA DORTMUND 3
(OCTOBER 31, 1956)

The match itself was irrelevant - although Birmingham City did play well - but the occasion was significant. When Birmingham City drew 3-3 with Borussia Dortmund of West Germany in October 1956, St Andrew's was able to boast floodlights for the first time. The stadium, which had opened on Boxing Day in 1906, did without artificial light for half a century.

Birmingham were so pleased to be entering the world of floodlights that they produced a special programme for the occasion. Abandoning the usual blue-dominated cover, the club opted for gold. It remains one of the club's rarest post-War programmes.

Alex Govan opened Birmingham's account and Brian 'Orrible' Orritt scored twice on a memorable evening. Dortmund, who were one of the best teams in Europe at that time, played attractive football and belied the perception that Germans are all about ruthless efficiency. The two clubs forged a good relationship that lasted for a while.

More than 45,000 people attended the match - an official attendance was not required and, therefore, not recorded - and St Andrew's had never looked better. The floodlights themselves were advanced for their time (four pylons, at each corner of the stadium, measuring 114 feet high). There were 30 lamps on each pylon, each lamp being 1500 Watts. The floodlights have changed since then, as has St Andrew's, but few who attended that match against Borussia Dortmund will forget it.

Workmen begin work on the new floodlights at St Andrew's

BIRMINGHAM CITY 2 INTERNAZIONALE 1 (APRIL 7, 1957)

The first Inter-cities Fairs Cup, which lasted from 1955 to 1958, was a tournament open to cities that had hosted trade fairs. Cities with more than one club sent representative teams (for example, London, who reached the first final).

A second tournament took place between 1958 and 1960, after which the competition was held on an annual basis. Prior to the mid-Sixties, qualification to the Fairs Cup had nothing to do with league position, meaning that Birmingham effectively became pioneers. The competition became the UEFA Cup in 1971.

Birmingham City had begun their 1955-58 Inter-cities Fairs Cup campaign with a goalless draw away to Internazionale in the San Siro Stadium, Milan, in May 1956. Only 8,000 people turned up. When the teams met at St Andrew's nearly a year later, 34,461 turned up. It was clear that interest was greater in England than it was in Italy.

These were not good times for Inter, while this was probably the strongest team in Birmingham's history. A Birmingham victory seemed inevitable, especially after Alex Govan scored twice. Lorenzi scored for Inter in the final two minutes but Birmingham's victory ensured that they topped the group - they also defeated Dinamo Zagreb twice - and qualified for the semi-finals.

Arthur Turner introduces joint manager Pat Beasley to the players, 1957

Supporters, shareholders and press prepare for the trip to Barcelona

BIRMINGHAM CITY 4
BARCELONA 3
(OCTOBER 23, 1957)

Surprisingly, interest in the Fairs Cup seemed to wane in Birmingham prior to the semi-finals. Only 30,791 attended the first leg of the semi-final against Barcelona - less than the crowd that witnessed the deciding group match against Internazionale - but there was still a unique atmosphere inside St Andrew's when the Spanish visitors took the field.

The match itself was marvellous, one of the most exciting to take place at St Andrew's. Eddie Brown gave Birmingham the lead in the first minute, before Tejada and Evaristo scored to put Barcelona in control. Bryan Orritt equalised for Birmingham in the 35th minute only for Martinez to restore Barcelona's advantage in the 40th minute.

But that only spurred Peter Murphy into action. The Birmingham wing-half made the scoreline 3-3 just before half-time and put his team 4-3 ahead with a goal on the hour mark. If the final 30 minutes were anti-climactic, that was

only to Birmingham's advantage. They looked good for progression into the final, against the London select team, and might have won on aggregate but for a goal by Kubala for Barcelona in the 86th minute of the second leg.

The 4-4 aggregate scoreline - no away goals ruling in those days - meant that the teams were forced to compete in a play-off, which took place at the St Jakob Stadium in Basle, Switzerland. Evaristo opened the scoring for Barcelona, Murphy equalised for Birmingham, but Kubala scored in the 83rd minute to send Barcelona into the final.

BIRMINGHAM CITY 0
BARCELONA 0
(MARCH 9, 1960)

St Andrew's played host to its first European final when Barcelona arrived in Birmingham to play the first leg of the 1960 Inter-cities Fairs Cup final. A crowd of 40,524 witnessed a tight goalless draw in which Birmingham struggled to break down a Barcelona midfield that seemed determined to keep a clean sheet.

Birmingham had scored freely in previous European matches that season and had won their semi-final against Union St Gilloise of Belgium 8-4 on aggregate. But Barcelona had style and cunning. Birmingham were on the wane and, at that point, were still fighting to avoid relegation into the Second Division. Barcelona were hot favourites and duly won the second leg 4-1 in front of more than 75,000 spectators in Spain.

Players and officials set to jet off to face Espanyol in the Fairs Cup, 1961

BIRMINGHAM CITY 2
AS ROMA 2
(SEPTEMBER 27, 1961)

The 1960-61 Inter-cities Fairs Cup final was held over until early in the 1961-62 season. That did not help Birmingham, who were lacking the strength in depth of the late-Fifties. But, as was usually the case in European matches, they saved their best performances for when the opposition came from the Continent.

This time, Birmingham's best football came in the final 12 minutes. Trailing 2-0, with Manfredini scoring twice for Roma, Birmingham bounced back to secure a draw with goals by Michael Hellawell (78th minute) and Bryan Orritt (85) to give themselves a chance in Rome two weeks after. But only 21,005 were there to witness the excitement.

Roma won the cup, however, with a controlled 2-0 victory in the Stadio Olympico on October 11, 1961. Fred Farmer set Roma on their way with an own goal after 56 minutes and Pestrin sealed Roma's victory with a last-minute strike.

But the second leg turned into a stormy affair. The Roma players did not like the tackling of the Birmingham players and the referee hardly helped matters with a fussy performance. At one stage, Luis Carniglia, the Roma trainer, squared up to Gil Merrick, the Birmingham goalkeeper, as the 50,000-plus spectators looked on in surprise.

BIRMINGHAM CITY 3
ASTON VILLA 1
(MAY 23, 1963)

Birmingham City officially won the League Cup with a goalless draw at Villa Park on May 27, 1963.

But they really won it on a memorable evening at St Andrew's four days before. It was not in keeping with the nature of their league form, which was wretched for the most part. Indeed, Birmingham only avoided relegation with a 3-2 victory against Leicester City on the final day of the season. Leicester, the FA Cup finalists, probably had their mind on other matters.

The League Cup suffered an uneasy beginning. In 1963, the competition did not provide a European place for the winners and the final did not take place at Wembley. Before 1967, the final was a two-legged affair.

The larger clubs, like Manchester United, did not bother to take part in the League Cup until the late-Sixties.

Birmingham's hopes of winning the competition seemed slim enough. They had lost 4-0 away to Villa just two months before and were not expected to improve. Surprisingly, then, they produced easily their best performance of the season with a fine display of attacking football.

In front of 31,580, Villa did not know what had hit them. In the 14th minute, after outplaying Villa from the kick-off, Ken Leek scored a fine

Players are mobbed after Blues beat Sheffield United 3-0 at St Andrew's to retain their place in Division One, April 1964

goal. The move involved Malcolm Beard, Terry Hennessey, Jimmy Harris and Bertie Auld. It was from Auld's cross that Leek scored with a fierce shot.

Against the run of play, Villa equalised through Bobby Thomson, who would later sign for Blues. Birmingham deservedly regained the lead in the 52nd minute with Leek scoring again, while Jimmy Bloomfield scored the third in the 66th minute with a shot that went in off a post. Birmingham might have scored more and there was a worry among the supporters that a 3-1 lead might not be good enough for the return leg at Villa Park.

But whereas the Birmingham strikers produced the goods in the first leg, it was the defenders who produced the goods in the second. The goalless draw ensured that Birmingham won the competition - the only leading trophy in their history.

BIRMINGHAM CITY 5
MANCHESTER UNITED 1
(NOVEMBER 4, 1978)

Birmingham City were bottom of the First Division table, without a victory, when they played Manchester United at St Andrew's. Relegation was already a probability. Birmingham had lost 10 of their opening 13 matches, scoring just seven goals. Jim Smith, the Birmingham manager, had already used 22 players and the four defenders seemed to change from match to match.

Stability, like confidence, was lacking. And yet, the arrival of Alberto Tarantini, a World Cup winner with Argentina four months before, suggested that Birmingham were thinking like a big club if not necessarily playing like one. Alan Buckley, a striker from Walsall, had also arrived.

But there was a feeling of inevitability when United opened the scoring in the 13th minute through Joe Jordan after Malcolm Page was dispossessed by Lou Macari. With 23,550 packed into St Andrew's, defeat hung in the air like a bad smell.

But it only took 10 minutes for the tide to turn. Kevin Dillon scored with a fierce shot that flew beyond the flailing arms of Paddy Roche. Buckley then scored, in the 32nd minute, heading home at the far post after good work by Don Givens and Tarantini and that man Buckley scored again just before half-time. United committed men forward and this left gaps at the back. Birmingham were grateful and they completed the rout with further goals by Givens and Jimmy Calderwood.

If only Birmingham could have maintained their fine form in this match. By February 13, when they lost 1-0 away to Liverpool, Birmingham's record in the First Division made bleak reading. Played 25, won 2, drawn 4, lost 19. There was slight improvement after that but not significant enough for Birmingham to avoid relegation. They finished in 21st position - despite winning their final match of the season, 3-1 away to Queens Park Rangers.

Alan Buckley heads home in the 5-1 rout of Manchester United in November, 1978. Above: Alberto Tarantini

Aerial action from the second city derby at St Andrew's, circa 1982

BIRMINGHAM CITY 3
ASTON VILLA 0
(DECEMBER 27, 1982)

Aston Villa were the European champions, but at St Andrew's on a grim December afternoon, just seven months after they won the trophy, Villa's decline began. Noel Blake, Ian Handysides and Mick Ferguson scored the Birmingham goals on a day that will live long in the memories of those who were privileged to be at St Andrew's that day. A crowd of 43,864 witnessed this remarkable event.

Tony Morley, who would later play for Birmingham, was still a Villa winger and England international. Like his team-mates, and the Villa supporters, he was stunned that the European champions could barely claim that they were the best team in the West Midlands.

"I think we realised that Villa were in decline that day we lost to Birmingham," Morley said. "I was on the substitutes' bench that day and it was amazing to think that we had won the European Cup just a few months before. Birmingham had a spring in their step and this match proved all this talk about the form book going out of the window for derbies. But it went deeper than that. In later years, when Villa were relegated, you could see that the decline had set in the year we won the European Cup. That match at Birmingham was terrible from our point of view. It was as if we had everything to lose and nothing to gain. Birmingham were not just playing their local rivals, they were playing the European champions. I cannot imagine a better incentive for them."

BIRMINGHAM CITY 4
IPSWICH TOWN 1 - AET
(JANUARY 31, 2001)

Probably the most dramatic match at St Andrew's ended late into the night as Birmingham City, of the Football League, defeated Ipswich Town, of the Premiership, to secure a place in the final of the League Cup. It needed extra time, it needed a remarkable display of fortitude, but Birmingham defeated Ipswich Town 4-1 on the night (4-2 on aggregate) to secure a place with Liverpool at the Millennium Stadium in Cardiff.

Two goals from Geoff Horsfield led the way on a wonderful night for Trevor Francis's team. Goals either side of the break by Martin Grainger and Horsfield reversed Ipswich's 1-0 lead from the first leg. Birmingham's advantage lasted less than a minute though as James Scowcroft scored, but Horsfield and Andrew Johnson then struck in extra time to assure an historic night for Birmingham.

If the 90 minutes at St Andrew's was stressful for the Birmingham supporters, the extra 30-minute period is one that will live long in the memory. Seven minutes into extra time, Trevor Francis sent on Johnson and the shape of the match changed. It was Horsfield, though, who struck the blow.

Danny Sonner's astute pass caught the defence square and Horsfield took the ball in his stride before stroking it precisely across Richard Wright into the far corner of the goal.

Johnson added the final blow when, with three minutes remaining, Wright made a horrible hash of a kick, allowing the substitute to roll the ball into the unguarded goal.

More surprising was Birmingham's impressive performance against Liverpool in the final. With the teams level at 1-1 after extra time, the penalty shootout favoured the more experienced players of Liverpool, but, even in defeat, Birmingham claimed a moral victory.

Geoff Horsfield shoots past Ipswich Town goalkeeper Richard Wright

Celebrations during the League Cup semi-final, second leg against Ipswich Town

Geoff Horsfield (top) and Michael Johnson are mobbed as Blues book a place in a major final for the first time in 38 years

BIRMINGHAM CITY 3
ASTON VILLA 0
(SEPTEMBER 16, 2002)

It was a night for Birmingham City to cherish and one for Peter Enckelman to forget. While Birmingham coasted to a derby victory at St Andrew's, the Aston Villa goalkeeper was left to contemplate a freakish mistake that effectively sealed the match.

This was the first league derby since December 1987 and it was worth the wait. With Birmingham leading thanks to a first-half strike by Clinton Morrison, Enckelman allowed a throw-in by Olof Mellberg to skid under his studs and roll into the goal. It doubled the lead for Steve Bruce's men at a crucial time and paved the way for Geoff Horsfield to score a third soon after.

It was an open, passionate derby and one that saw Birmingham rise to the occasion. Villa had their moments but, in the final analysis, crumbled when the situation demanded composure. Villa had only conceded three goals in their previous five matches but were found lacking at key moments.

Birmingham were more direct and, initially, the more confident. It was inevitable, then, that they should take the lead. In the 31st minute, Jeff Kenna hooked the ball towards the penalty spot and, with Villa's offside trap failing, Robbie Savage was able to touch the ball to Morrison whose right-footed shot from close range beat Enckelman.

Darius Vassell thought he had equalised in the 57th minute but, before his crisp volley beat Nico Vaesen, the Villa striker was flagged for offside.

The decision did not meet with the approval of Graham Taylor, the Villa manager, who, suggesting an injustice, argued long enough to earn a rebuke from David Elleray, the Middlesex-based referee who had not endeared himself to the visiting supporters.

And then, in the 74th minute, came one of the most bizarre goals seen in 100 years at St Andrew's. Mellberg threw the ball back to

Clinton Morrison fires home the opener from close range against Aston Villa, September 2003

Enckelman and the Villa goalkeeper inexplicably allowed the ball to bobble under his studs and trickle into the goal.

There was a minute of confusion when a number of players from each team surrounded Elleray, but the conclusion was inevitable. Enckelman had unwittingly put Birmingham two goals ahead.

From Villa's point of view, the third goal was also self-inflicted. Alpay Ozalan lost the ball close to his penalty area and allowed Horsfield, a substitute, to beat the Villa goalkeeper with a low shot from 10 yards.

One only had to consider the difference in the reactions of Enckelman and Horsfield to sum up the story of this surreal match.

Clinton Morrison is mobbed after his derby strike (above), while Geoff Horsfield rams home the third goal to seal Villa's fate at St Andrew's

BIRMINGHAM CITY 3
SOUTHAMPTON 2
(APRIL 21, 2003)

Birmingham City were still not sure of avoiding relegation when they went into this match at home to Southampton. With Christophe Dugarry in the team, they need not have worried. The former France international striker, a World Cup winner with France five years before, was so good that even the Southampton supporters applauded him.

There are observers who believe that his performance here was the best by a Birmingham City player at St Andrew's.

For all that Eddie Brown did for Birmingham in the Fifties and Trevor Francis did in the Seventies, they never came close to the heights that Dugarry reached on this spring afternoon in 2003.

Dugarry scored twice but did much more. His inspiration was such that his team-mates, 10 mere mortals, seemed to be there merely as bit-part players.

Southampton might have won had Dugarry not been in the team - and Birmingham might have endured relegation. But Dugarry was in the team. And Dugarry was brilliant.

Anders Svensson gave Southampton the lead early in the first half and the visitors seemed set for victory.

But all the action came in the final 15 minutes. Dugarry equalised in the 75th minute, Brett Ormerod restored Southampton's lead two minutes later, only for Bryan Hughes to make the scoreline two-apiece. And then, in the 82nd minute, Dugarry emerged to send the home supporters into paroxysms of delight.

The emergence of Stern John as a late substitute helped Birmingham and liberated Dugarry. But Dugarry was untouchable that day and, consequently, Birmingham avoided relegation with relative ease. We did not know it then but, while Dugarry still had 11 months left of his Birmingham career, he would never again be as effective.

Christophe Dugarry heads home the winner against Southampton, April 2003

Dugarry celebrates with team-mates and coaching staff following his equaliser against Saints (top), while visiting manager Gordon Strachan takes evasive action as the Frenchman retrieves the ball

BIRMINGHAM CITY 2 LIVERPOOL 0 (FEBRUARY 12, 2005)

Was this the finest performance by a Birmingham City team? Probably. There is little doubt that Liverpool were below par but that was partly because Birmingham were so good. Indeed, Birmingham had defeated Liverpool at Anfield the previous November.

This match at St Andrew's was effectively won and lost in the first half when Walter Pandiani scored with a penalty and Julian Gray struck with a volley at the far post after a cross by Jermaine Pennant.

Emile Heskey, previously of Liverpool, was untouchable on this occasion. The Liverpool players paid him the ultimate compliment by panicking whenever he went near the ball. There are those who question Heskey's international credentials but this was a day when he looked world class.

Liverpool were in bad shape at the time - even Steven Gerrard looked jaded and disillusioned - and they did not look like a team that would, three months later, win the European Cup against AC Milan in Istanbul.

This was the day when Birmingham looked as if they could cope without Robbie Savage, who had moved to Blackburn Rovers only a few weeks before.

Alas, this performance flattered to deceive. Birmingham were already in decline and, 14 months later, would endure relegation. But, for 90 minutes, Birmingham outplayed and outperformed the team that were destined to become the European champions.

Walter Pandiani celebrates his penalty against Liverpool - while Julian Gray wheels away after volleying the second (below)

And two INFAMOUS games . . .

The look on Maik Taylor's face says it all on a night to forget against Liverpool

BIRMINGHAM CITY 0 LIVERPOOL 7 (MARCH 21, 2006)

Birmingham City's record against Liverpool since the arrival of Steve Bruce was impressive. The teams had drawn both of their Premiership matches that season - 2-2 at St Andrew's in September, 1-1 at Anfield in February - and Birmingham had defeated Liverpool twice the previous season. But, by March 2006, Birmingham were slipping alarmingly.

Although this was an FA Cup sixth-round tie, this was the evening when, suddenly, relegation from the Premiership looked likely. Liverpool could hardly believe their luck.

Birmingham were effectively out of the competition in the fifth minute when, courtesy of poor defending, they allowed Liverpool to score twice from inside the six-yard box.

Sami Hyypia and Peter Crouch scored the goals and the final 85 minutes was all about damage limitation.

Crouch scored again in the 39th minute and Birmingham were so poor that even the inconsistent Fernando Morientes scored for Liverpool, on the hour mark. Riise scored the fifth, Olivier Tebily's own goal made it six and Djibril Cisse scored the seventh in the last minute.

Not many Birmingham supporters witnessed the final two goals.

With defeat assured, St Andrew's was starting to empty at half-time. Liverpool went on to win the FA Cup. Birmingham would slip into the Coca-Cola Football League Championship.

BIRMINGHAM CITY 0
NEWCASTLE UNITED 0
(APRIL 29, 2006)

Ian Clarkson, a Birmingham City captain during the early-Nineties, was a journalist for The Birmingham Post when the team slipped out of the Premiership with a goalless draw against Newcastle United. As a match, there was nothing memorable here. As an occasion, it was depressing; perhaps the worst since the days of the Third Division in the late-Eighties, when Clarkson was a young player.

'When Birmingham City's relegation was confirmed there were no jeers and no vitriol, rather a wave of apathy, resignation and general indifference,' Clarkson wrote. 'Supporters had strained every sinew, as had every single player against Newcastle, but it wasn't good enough.

'That has been the fundamental problem for Birmingham all season. Undoubtedly, relegation rivals Portsmouth have been granted fortuitous penalties, snatched late goals and faced ostensibly reserve teams on more than one occasion during their own version of the "Great Escape" but it would be folly to blame Blues' relegation on sheer bad luck.

'The "we-wuz-robbed" brigade were out in force again on Saturday after television replays clearly showed Newcastle defender Celestine Babayaro handled a Damien Johnson cross to deny Emile Heskey an opportunity on goal. However, Birmingham missed presentable opportunities to procure a vital win and had to settle for a fatal goalless draw.

'The fact that Wigan, whose loss against Portsmouth condemned Blues to Championship football, had a perfectly good "goal" disallowed only rubbed salt into an already festering wound. A plethora of injuries have undoubtedly hindered Steve Bruce but the cold hard facts are that Blues just have not been good enough.'

Some would say that Clarkson was too harsh but his comments seemed to reflect the mood among the majority of supporters. Alas, the Premiership does not lie. Birmingham's relegation was confirmed at 5pm that sunny Saturday afternoon. Within an hour, St Andrew's resembled a funeral procession. The stadium was built for much more stimulating occasions.

Kenny Cunningham and Matthew Sadler contemplate relegation following the 0-0 draw with Newcastle

BLUES BROTHERS

TWO of Birmingham City's favourite sons made a lasting impact on life with Blues during the 1970s. Trevor Francis and Joe Gallagher (second and third left) were to take Blues on the road to better things. It was to prove a colourful journey

If Birmingham City were at their best in the mid-Fifties, and their most expensive at the start of the 21st century, they were surely at their most exciting in the Seventies. This was the era of Trevor Francis, Bob Hatton, Gordon Taylor, Alan Campbell, Bob Hatton and Joe Gallagher. This was the era of large crowds, of great atmospheres, of nationwide rebellion and, at St Andrew's, of no success.

It is a common theme in the history of the club. Birmingham can win football matches, can win friends, but they cannot win trophies. "Birmingham teams tend to give the fans hope and then, at the final hurdle, let everybody down," Gallagher says. "I can't think of any other big clubs who have underachieved quite as spectacularly as Birmingham. Before I signed, they always seemed to be in one semi-final or another. In the Seventies, when I was there, we reached the FA Cup semi-final twice and still couldn't reach the final at Wembley. After I left, when Trevor Francis was manager, we seemed to lose in the First Division play-off semi-finals every year. And even when we reached the League Cup final, in 2001, we lost to Liverpool on penalties."

Such are the trials and tribulations of supporting Birmingham, or, in the case of Joe Gallagher, of playing for Birmingham. He was a defender who spent the whole of the Seventies at St Andrew's. He caught the end of the Stan Cullis era in 1970 and lasted until the Jim Smith era in the early Eighties. Though the money was not great ("I earned £280 a week in 1980-81, my final season"), Gallagher says it was a good time to be playing in the First Division. "I am sometimes asked if I regret that I did not earn the sums that

players earn in 2006," he says. "And I say, no, I don't regret it. I played at a time when it was a privilege to be part of a great Birmingham team. I wouldn't have missed playing with Trevor Francis for the world. We were of a similar age. He was nine months older than me and, in 1970, we were both 16. It was an exciting time for both of us, although Trevor was way ahead of me. He made his debut in 1970 and I had to wait until 1973. But we lived the dream together. We lived our fantasies."

Gallagher was the Liverpool supporter who turned down Bill Shankly. "I had the chance to join Liverpool, Everton or Birmingham City. Yes, I was a Liverpool fan, but I wanted to make the

Joe Gallagher, taken during the pre-season photocall of 1980-81

grade and I thought that Birmingham would offer me the best chance. So I turned up at New Street Station, arse hanging out of my trousers, to sign for Birmingham. It was 1970 and I couldn't believe that I'd turned down Bill Shankly. And I don't have any regrets at all because St Andrew's was buzzing in the Seventies. Absolutely buzzing.

"I remember meeting Freddie Goodwin, who had just taken over as manager from Stan Cullis. I was just a boy and I was in awe of this man. He was an inspiration to me. Of course, at the time, I'd never worked under another manager, so I knew no different. But, by the time I'd finished my career, I'd played for 16 managers and Goodwin stands out as one of the best. I hadn't made the first team when the team secured promotion to the First Division in 1972. But that didn't matter much to me because I was so happy to be part of the club. I remember St Andrew's throbbing in those days, with large crowds on the terraces, and great players on the pitch. Goodwin signed Roger Hynd, a strong defender, Alan Campbell and Gordon Taylor. And, of course, we had Trevor Francis, who was the Wayne Rooney of his time."

Hyperbole? Not so, for Francis was a player 10 years ahead of his time. Gallagher was in the stands, still too young for the first team, when Birmingham City played Bolton Wanderers at St Andrew's on February 20, 1971. "He was still two months short of his 17th birthday," Gallagher says. "But he played like a man, destroying the Bolton defenders and scoring all the goals in a 4-0 victory. It was amazing stuff, truly amazing. And because I was the same age as Trevor,

Young hopefuls...Trevor Francis (left) and his fellow apprentices meet Birmingham City manager Stan Cullis and coach Don Dorman

and spent a lot of time with him, I could feel his joy better than most. The funny thing is, Trevor did not even complete the match. Goodwin took him off late on, presumably to protect him. Well, Trevor was only 16. The manager would often leave him out. Nobody was surprised."

There were bad teams in the Second Division - that was inevitable - but there were no bad teams in the First Division. Birmingham reached the FA Cup semi-finals in 1972 but lost emphatically to Leeds United. Birmingham did win the FA Cup third-place play-off against Stoke City at St Andrew's at the start of the 1972-73 season and finished the campaign in a respectable 10th position. The most memorable match at St Andrew's that season was the 2-1 victory against Liverpool, with Bob Latchford and Bob Hatton scoring the goals. Liverpool

won the League Championship just three weeks later. Birmingham finished the season with seven victories and a draw from eight matches. "I was still on the outside looking in at that point," Gallagher says. "But I knew that the 1973-74 season would be significant. I could just feel it."

Gallagher made his debut for Birmingham against Arsenal at Highbury in October 1973. Birmingham lost 1-0. His first home match was against Everton two weeks later. Birmingham lost 2-0. But these were good insights into the beautiful frustrations of life in the First Division. By the time Gallagher settled into the starting line-up, Birmingham were involved in a fight for their First Division survival. "By springtime, every match seemed to be like a cup final," Gallagher remembers. "Then we

played Manchester United in the middle of March at St Andrew's. At the time, the talk was that whoever won would survive and whoever lost would be relegated. Manchester United were having a tough time then. George Best had just left for the final time and they were running out of good players. Amazing to think that they had won the European Cup just six years before. Anyway, we won 1-0 and I scored the goal. It was a mis-kick but one that was good enough to beat Alex Stepney. I suppose you could say that, indirectly, I sent Manchester United into the Second Division. Their relegation was confirmed just a few weeks afterwards and I think we survived by just one point, ahead of Southampton. Our victory against Norwich City at St Andrew's on the final day of the season was so crucial. It was a close-run thing, I can tell you. So tense but so exciting."

Joe Gallagher shows his anguish after former Blues striker Bob Latchford nets for Everton past his grounded brother, Birmingham goalkeeper Dave in January 1975

Despite this perceived success, however, Freddie Goodwin's days as the Birmingham manager were drawing to a close. In 1975, Birmingham reached the FA Cup semi-finals again but they continued to struggle in the First Division. Birmingham seemed to scrape through each round of the FA Cup, defeating Luton Town and Chelsea away, Walsall and Middlesbrough at home. "When the draw was made for the semi-finals, it was between Birmingham, Fulham, Ipswich Town and West Ham United," Gallagher recalls. "I can remember sitting in my car, waiting for my girlfriend, and hoping that we would get Fulham. They were a mid-table Second Division club and, let's face it, we knew that everyone wanted to draw Fulham. When the draw paired us with Fulham, I punched my fist into the air. I honestly believed it was a guaranteed place in the final. Well, we played Fulham at Hillsborough and they took

the lead with a good goal. But I equalised with a fine shot on the turn, although I did not see the ball hit the back of the net. It finished 1-1 and, in the dressing room afterwards, we were dejected. We had played so badly. The only consolation was that we could not possibly be as bad in the replay at Maine Road four days later. Well, we did improve, but we still lost when Fulham scored in the last minute of extra time. I was heartbroken. I didn't know it then but that was my one and only chance to play in the FA Cup final."

Goodwin left when Birmingham picked up just two points from their opening seven First Division matches of 1975-76. It set the scene and Birmingham spent the entire campaign in yet another battle to avoid relegation, although Willie Bell, who took over from Goodwin, did make improvements. "Willie Bell was just about the quietest manager you could

ever wish to play for," Gallagher says. "I mean, he would never shout, even when things were going badly, or when somebody made a bad mistake. He was softly spoken and players responded to that. I think he was just what we needed at the time. I felt sorry for Freddie Goodwin but I don't know what the situation was between him and the club directors. Whatever, this felt like a new era and there was improvement in 1976-77. You could sense it at the start of the season, even though we only drew our first two matches."

It was the third match of that season which provided Gallagher with the most memorable game he had witnessed as a player or spectator at St Andrew's. He was playing in the match, it was against Liverpool, and everything just seemed to go right for Birmingham. "That was a great day," Gallagher remarked. "We defeated

Liverpool 2-1. Trevor Francis had scored for us, it was 1-1, and then I scored. My goal came from a free-kick routine that had never worked in training yet worked here for the first time. After I scored, I ran towards my mum and dad, who were down from Liverpool and were near to the corner flag between the Railway End and the Main Stand. I did my Roger Hunt celebration. When I saw my mum, I was surprised to see that she was wearing a red hat, just as most of the Liverpool fans were wearing red hats. I think she was just keeping warm, rather than making a statement as to who she supported. We finished 13th that season but the significance of our victory against Liverpool became obvious in May when they won the European Cup,

the League Championship and reached the FA Cup final. We did what the best teams in Europe couldn't do - we defeated Liverpool."

The 1976-77 campaign was encouraging enough but Birmingham began the 1977-78 season with four straight defeats. Willie Bell could not survive that and was encouraged to vacate his position as manager in September 1977. Gallagher recalls: "I liked Willie a lot. He had been a good player and I remember watching him play in the 1965 FA Cup final for Leeds United against Liverpool at Wembley. There was certainly nothing in his make-up, when he was the manager of Birmingham, to suggest that he would eventually move

to America to join a religious cult. You could not see that coming. But he just went to Virginia, I think, and did some coaching in his spare time. It is a strange story but these things happen. With hindsight, perhaps he was already involved in some religious activity when he was still manager of Birmingham. I don't know but I think English football missed him."

Bell's replacement was the most decorated manager in English football history. Sir Alf Ramsey led England to victory in the 1966 World Cup final and joined the board of directors at St Andrew's in January 1976. He took over in September 1977 and steadied the ship in unspectacular fashion, as Gallagher ▶

Birmingham City in training at St Andrew's, with Joe fifth in line

The players line-up alongside a TR7 - this was given to Kenny Burns and the rest of the Birmingham City team after they scored 6 goals in a game (left)

Action from Blues v Walsall in the early 1970s (right)

Birmingham City manager Willie Bell and secretary Alan Instone (second left) pictured with new signings Keith Bertschin (left) and Tony Towers (right) - July 1977

Paul Hendrie lies injured as Bob Hatton takes exception to Pat Howard's challenge against Newcastle United - the linesman and goalkeeper Ian McFaul act as peacemakers!

Bob Latchford beats Martin Peters to a high ball in the Tottenham Hotspur penalty area, with Bob Hatton (centre) and Spurs' Alan Gilzean waiting for the flick header, early 1970s (above); police in force at the St Andrew's ticket office, 1970s (below)

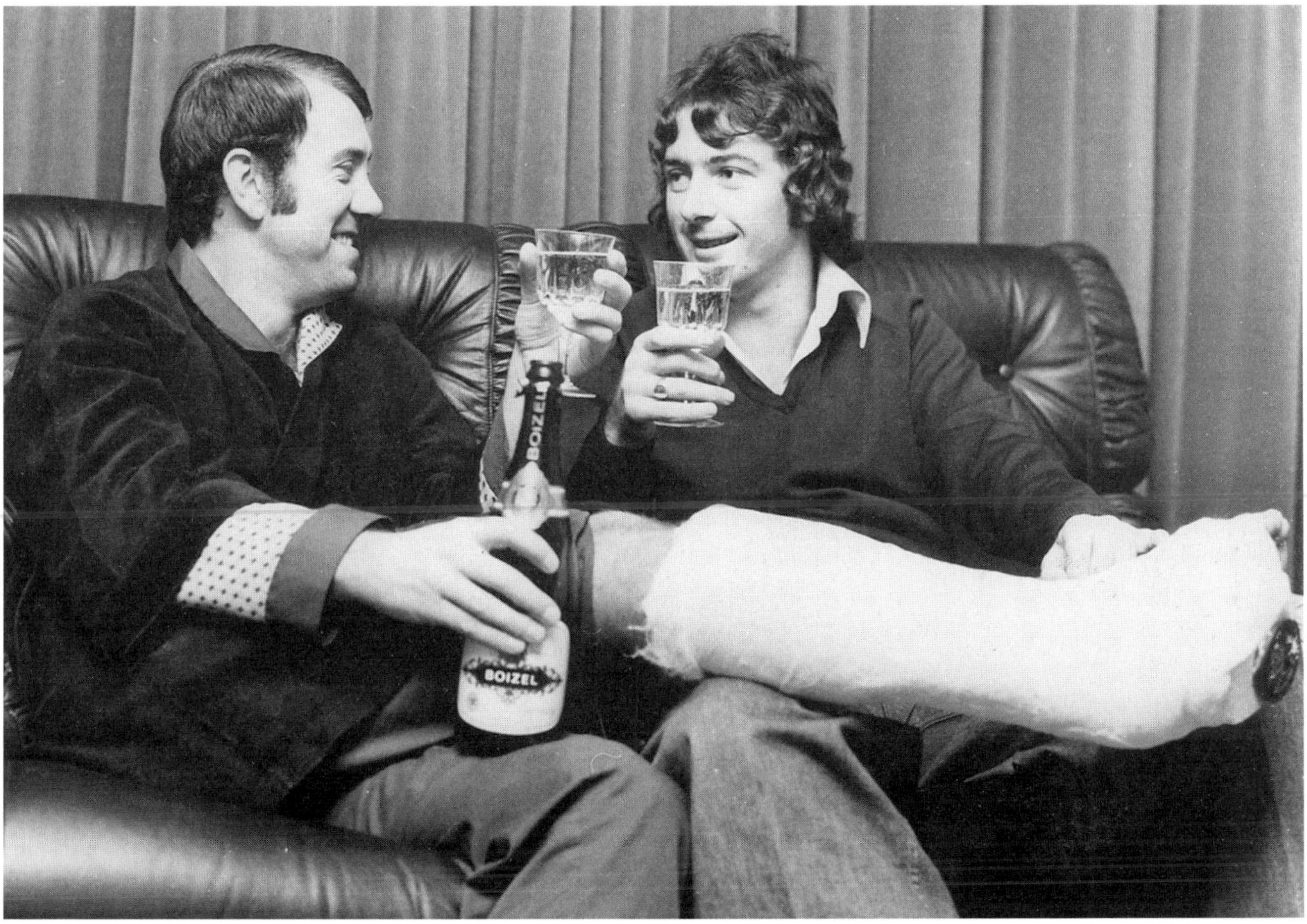

Howard Kendall and Trevor Francis share a glass, October 1976. Blues skipper Kendall was recovering from an operation to clear up a nagging tendon injury while Francis had just made his 200th appearance for City against QPR

Kevan Broadhurst on target for Blues, mid-1970s

recalls: "It was amazing, really. Like everyone of my age group, I watched on television England win the 1966 World Cup. Suddenly, here was the man who won the World Cup turning up at St Andrew's and now he was my manager.

'It was an odd arrangement, really, because he was so famous, so experienced, yet it did not seem right. He would turn up to training with his nice suit, a shirt and tie, and just watch us. It could be pouring with rain and he would still be there. Then, afterwards, he would just talk quietly to us. He was a gentleman, was Sir Alf, but I am not sure if the experiment worked. I think he had lost that way of connecting with the players on the training ground. We did OK as a team, nothing spectacular, but there was never a feeling that Sir Alf was there on a long-term basis. I was not surprised when he resigned at the start of 1978. Sir Alf would always be on hand to talk to you. I remember once my mistake gave a goal away against Manchester United at Old Trafford. It was when Sir Alf was a director and not the manager.

Willie Bell was clearly unhappy with me but Sir Alf sat me down and said, 'don't worry, son, I could see that you were trying to keep the ball in play and start a Birmingham move.

'I know how you feel. I would have tried the same thing myself'.

That was great man-management and I have never forgotten that. I made the mistake but Sir Alf saw the positive side of what I had tried to do."

Ramsey's replacement was a man significantly different in looks and personality. Jim Smith, bald, brash, loud, interesting and experienced, took over in March 1978. Birmingham were never in danger of losing their First Division status that season, not with Trevor Francis in the kind of form that saw him score in seven successive matches that spring. But Francis was clearly becoming disillusioned with Birmingham's failures. By the end of the season, rumours were rife that Francis had asked for a transfer. It was as if he had become bigger than the club. But before Francis had a chance to leave, Birmingham attracted the services of an even more successful and famous player. His name was Alberto Tarantini

The protests are in vain as Aston Villa are awarded a penalty - although Trevor Francis would have the final word for Blues...

Joe Gallagher (far left) and Trevor Francis (far right) - hard at work during training

and, in June 1978, he won a World Cup winners' medal as part of the Argentina team. When he signed for Birmingham in 1978, the English game was aghast with surprise. Tarantini was skilful, hard, brave and versatile - or so it seemed. In fact, as soon as he arrived at St Andrew's, he looked no more cut out for the rigours of First Division football than a trout in hot petrol. It was perhaps the most misconceived transfer of the Seventies. A defender who could not defend; an Argentinian who could not pass; a hard man who could not tackle. What was all that about?

"In terms of the name and his reputation, Alberto Tarantini was incredible," Gallagher claims. "But in reality, the whole thing did not work out. Who am I, this average First Division defender? Who am I, to criticise this man who has played dozens of matches for Argentina, who has won a World Cup winners' medal? So I don't like to criticise him. But I would say that he seemed unable to do the things you would expect from somebody with his experience and reputation. The thing is, he was such a nice man. He really was. I used to drive him home after training every day and I enjoyed his company. He lived near to Sutton Coldfield and we would have interesting conversations. All along I was thinking to myself, 'here is this World Cup winner and he hasn't even got a bloody car'. From a personal point of view, I was sad to see him leave. From a professional point of view, he was not what we needed at that time."

Tarantini left in the spring of 1979. Birmingham were left wondering how they could employ a manager - Sir Alf Ramsey - who had won the World Cup yet failed at St Andrew's, and a player who also won the World Cup and failed at the same ground. By contrast, Jim Smith had made his name in lower-league football, but even he was finding that Birmingham were in decline. Relegation to the Second Division was confirmed a few weeks after Tarantini's last match for the club. Birmingham would begin the new decade outside the top flight. By then, Trevor Francis had left to join Nottingham Forest for £975,000. The fee was revealed to the media as being the first million-pound signing but the actual amount was short. Once Francis left, Birmingham were without their best significant player. Relegation was inevitable.

"There is nothing worse than relegation for a footballer," Gallagher says.

"There is this empty feeling, then a feeling of guilt for the supporters, then a whole summer where you are helpless. It is hard to argue with Trevor for leaving. He ended the season by scoring the winning goal for Nottingham Forest in the European Cup final, a couple of weeks after Birmingham were relegated. What a contrast in fortunes.

"For me, Francis is the best player in Birmingham's history. OK, people talk of Joe Bradford but he played in the Thirties, which was a different era. Trevor played in the era of the superstar and he never looked out of place. In fact, he was a superstar, certainly among Birmingham supporters."

But Gallagher, too, was coming towards the end of his career with Birmingham. He was still only 26 when the Eighties arrived but he was not the player of 1976-77. Then he was on the verge of making the full England squad.

Alas, in the summer of 1977, fate intervened. Gallagher had been a judge at a beauty contest in Northfield, Birmingham, and was driving home with his wife. Gallagher's car crashed in a field and all he remembers was that he could not feel a leg. "It was numb. I could not move it. Then I passed out. The next thing I knew I was in hospital. The first thing I heard was Tony Butler

(local radio personality) talking on his show and saying that Joe Gallagher's career is over because of a leg broken in six places. I was so upset. I telephoned my dad and he was upset, too. It turned out that my leg was only broken in two places and that I would be able to play again.

"Well, my comeback match was six months and six days later, which was pretty good going in those days. But I knew that I was never the same player after that.

"The broken leg was my jumping leg, so I was never as dominant in the air after that. I won an international cap for the England 'B' team against Australia in 1980 but I honestly believe I would have won full caps had it not been for the injury. In 1977, I was playing really well.

"There was talk that I might make the step-up to the full international squad. There were other young defenders but I really fancied my chances.

"But, hey, that's life. I am grateful that I played for a club I loved, in an era that I loved, and was fit and healthy. I always had a relationship with the supporters and that made me appreciate the career that I had. It kept my feet on the ground."

Gallagher left Birmingham in 1981 after more than a decade at St Andrew's.

The original plan was for Gallagher to join Wolverhampton Wanderers, with John Richards, a striker, moving in the opposite direction. "I did not want to join Wolves," Gallagher states.

"And I told Birmingham that. But they said that they needed John Richards badly. The swap deal never happened but I still moved to Wolves.

But I missed Birmingham, even years later when I played non-League football."

There was, Gallagher says, something special about St Andrew's. He did not regard the stadium as being pretty but there was an atmosphere about the place that inspired players.

"I remember when I played for Birmingham in the FA Youth Cup in the early Seventies. We played Tottenham Hotspur, who had Graeme Souness in their team.

"It was an amazing experience because I was only 16 or 17. Anyway, there must have been about 13,000 people at St Andrew's that night. In the first-team match before it, there was only about 14,000.

"Read into that what you will but the Birmingham fans have this ability to get behind you when it matters. Even now, when stadiums are all-seated and attendances are lower, you still get a nice atmosphere at St Andrew's.

"How could you fail when the crowd were on your side? That was how we felt in the Seventies. We had our bad times, sure, but there was also a lot of good football played at St Andrew's then.

"Enough of it was played by Birmingham for me to believe that we were a really attractive team in those days. The mid-Seventies team broke up too quickly.

"We might have achieved so much more for those supporters who deserved another major domestic trophy.

"What have we won?

"The League Cup. That was in 1963, when the competition was not taken as seriously as it is now.

"Birmingham must achieve a lot more. Hopefully they will do it before the club vacates St Andrew's."

Joe Gallagher rises highest, circa 1980

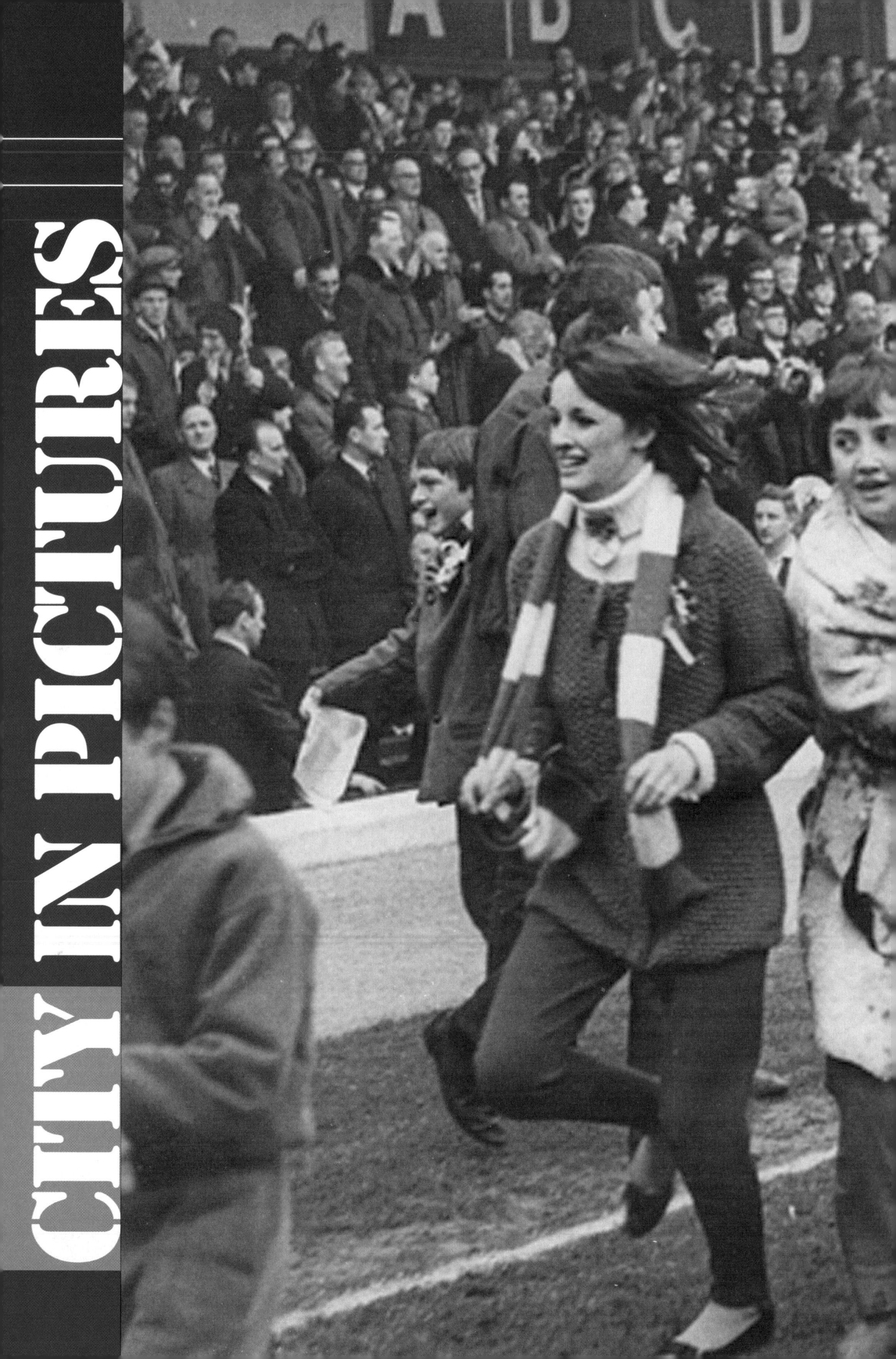

AN extensive trawl through the archives featuring Blues mascots, revolutions, snow fights, souvenirs, parachute jumps and Wembley days out - plus the odd bit of Birmingham City Football Club action at St Andrew's and elsewhere . . .

Above: Players and guests sit down to a banquet at the Park Lane Hotel, Piccadilly (date unknown).
Opposite page: Ken Green heads clear for Blues at St Andrew's, season 1951-52

Above: Birmingham City's mascots offer their support ahead of an FA Cup third-round tie against Fulham at Craven Cottage (date unknown). Opposite page, top: The Blues party leave Birmingham to play two games in the north (date unknown). Opposite page, bottom: Blues practice - Stewart scores from the penalty spot past the dive of Schofield (date unknown)

Above, top: Gordon Astall holds off Lindsay to bring Blues' second goal in the 5-1 victory over Everton - pictured left to right are Astall, Lindsay, Govan, Clinton and O'Neill (December, 1953).
Left: Fisher in a tussle with a Bradford full-back (date unknown).
Opposite page, top: Training seems unlikely due to ice. Left to right: Gil Merrick, Ken Rowley, Jim Dailey, Tony Blake, Ken Green and Tommy Briggs watch Bill Smith test the ground with a hammer (date unknown).
Opposite page, bottom: Ted Purdon opens the scoring against Fulham (date unknown

A. GOVAN

E. BROWN

N. KINSEY

G. MERRICK

J. NEWMAN

T. SMITH

G. ASTALL

L. BOYD

K. GREEN

J. HALL

P. MURPHY

BIRMINGHAM CITY 19 F.A. C

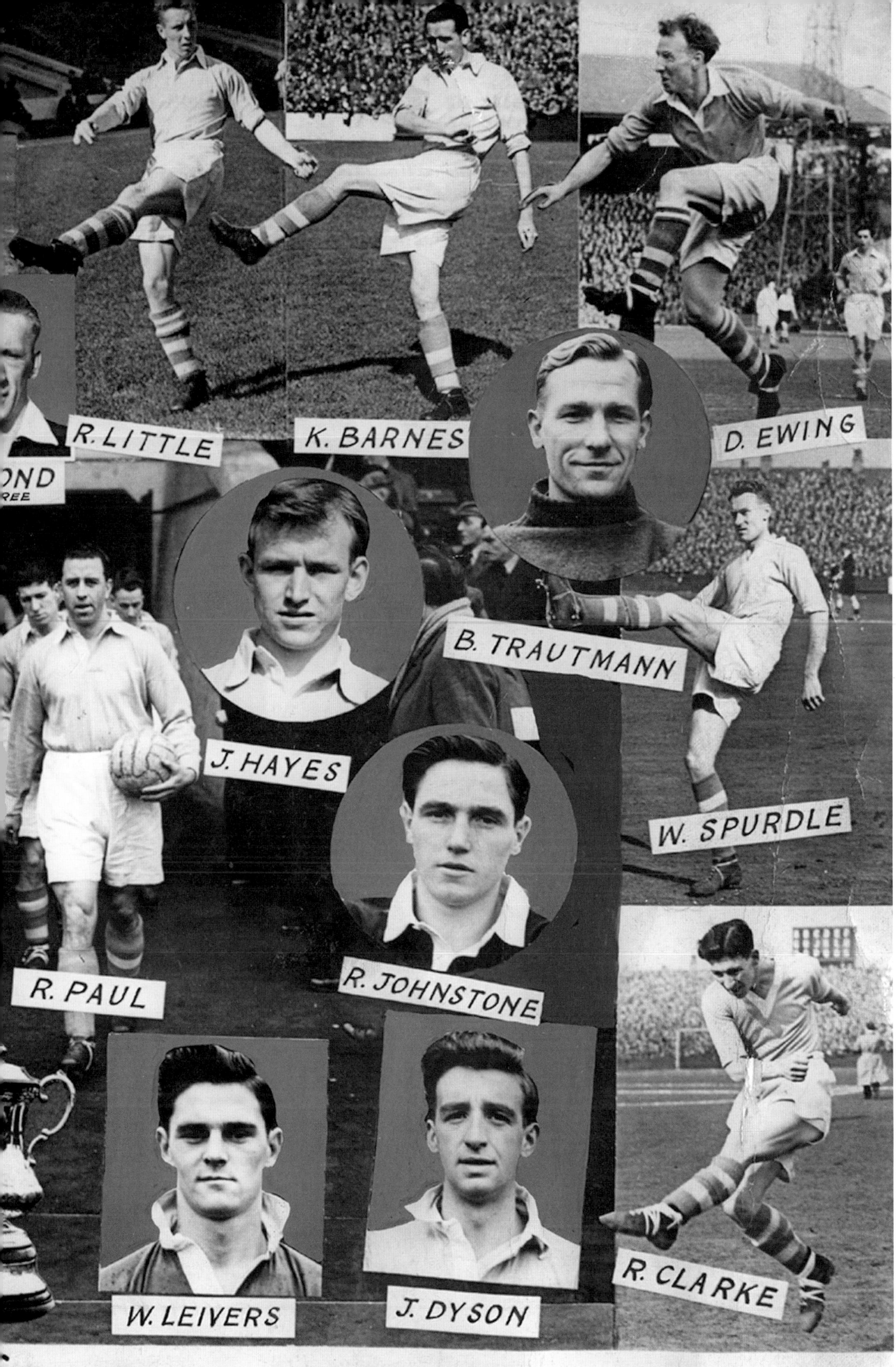
R. LITTLE
K. BARNES
D. EWING
OND
REE
B. TRAUTMANN
J. HAYES
W. SPURDLE
R. PAUL
R. JOHNSTONE
W. LEIVERS
J. DYSON
R. CLARKE

S
INAL **MANCHESTER CITY**

Previous page:
A 1956 FA Cup final preview pull-out taken from the Liverpool Echo, 05/05/56.

Above: Supporters enjoy the Wembley atmosphere before the final.
Left: Birmingham City players being presented to the Duke of Edinburgh

Above: Birmingham players make use of the weather conditions. Original caption: 'How to make a snowman, first take a footballer, South African variety preferred, cover with snow and get a living image of Ted Purdon' (1950s)

Team Photos - Above: Line-Up, circa early 1950s.
Left: February 1961.
Opposite page, top: Back row, left to right: Fairhurst, Smith, Green, Boyd, Merrick, Badham, Martin, Higgins, Shaw.
Front row: Stewart, Warhurst, Purdon, Brocklebank, Briggs, Murphy, Wardle.
Sitting on ground: Hall, Ferris.
Opposite page, bottom: Line-up, circa late 1950s

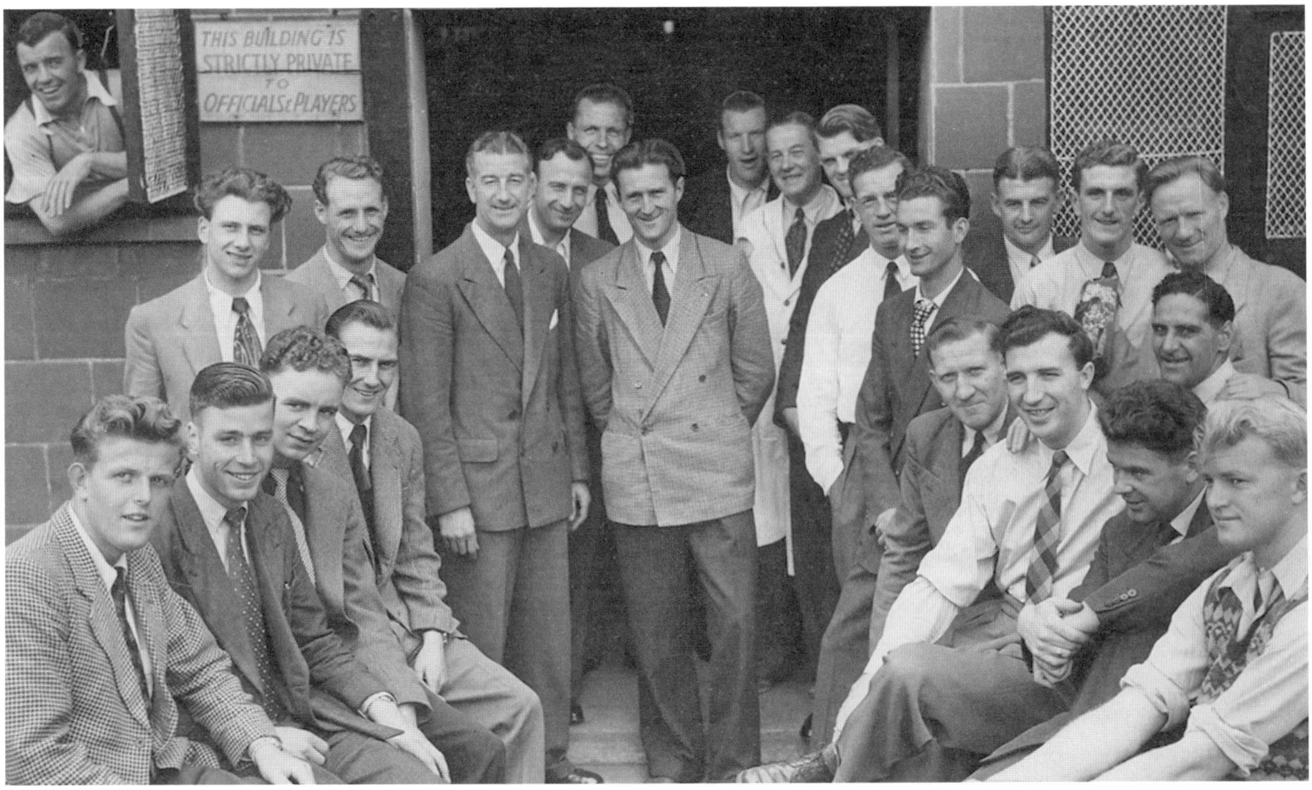
THIS BUILDING IS
STRICTLY PRIVATE
TO
OFFICIALS & PLAYERS

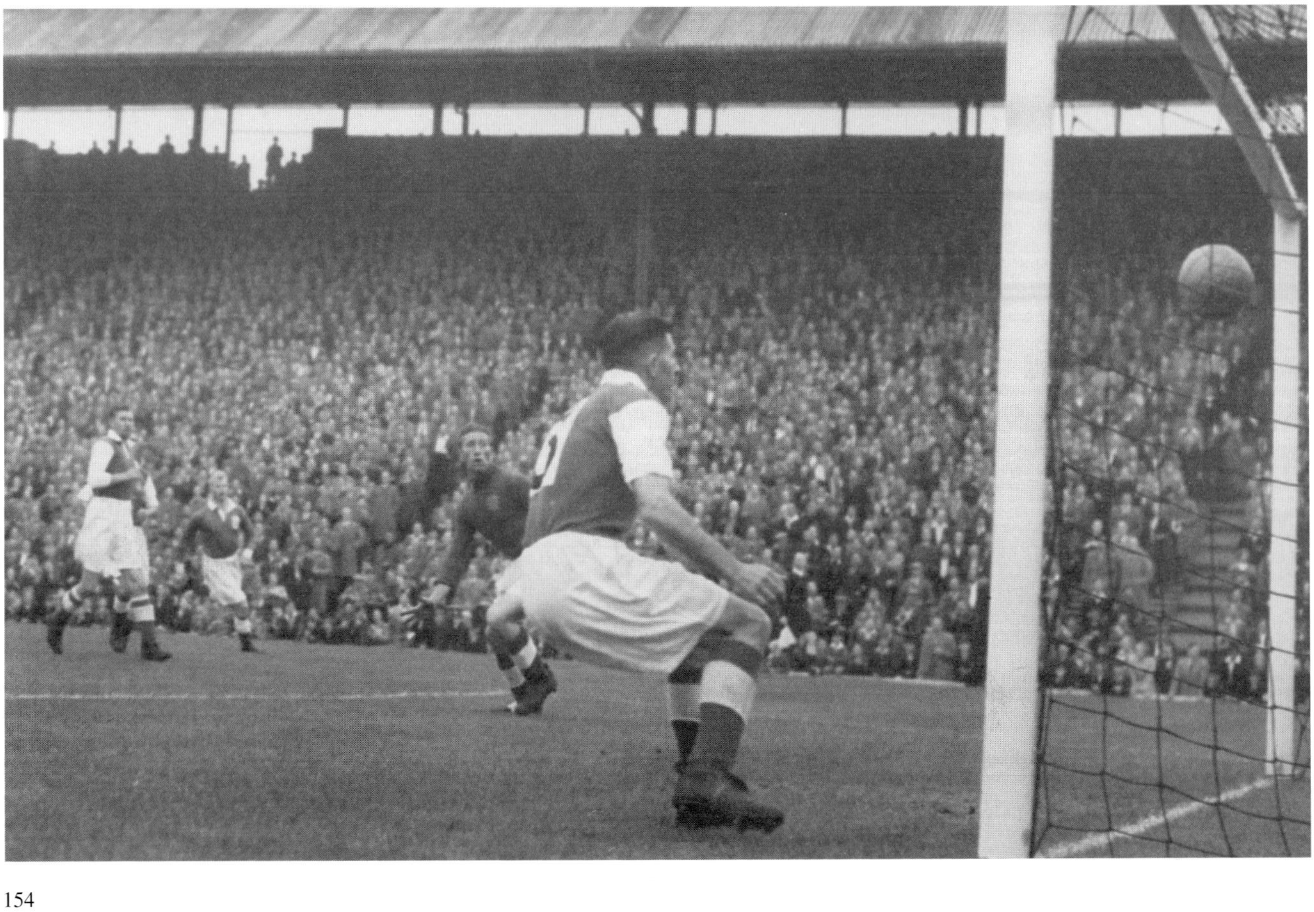

Left and bottom: Action
from Blues v Manchester
City at St Andrew's,
1957-58.
Opposite page, top:
The players are all smiles
as they report for training
- Jackie Stewart is leaning
out of the window (date
unknown).
Opposite page, bottom:
City v Plymouth Argyle -
and a goal for the home
side (date unknown)

BRIGGS · BAKER · MURPHY · McLAUGHLIN · STEWART · TRIGG · HUGHES

Above: Green - not captioned, and hidden by the goalkeeper, despatches this penalty for Blues (1950s - opposition unknown).
Below: A run round the track for some City players at St Andrew's (date unknown)

Above: Training the Blues way (date unknown). Below: The players report for training, 1957

Above: Members of the Blues squad show off mementos from a trip to Spain in 1958. Left to right are: Ray Shaw, Harry Hooper, Dick Neal, Eddie Brown, Peter Murphy and Trevor Smith.
Left: Warhurst's effort flashes just wide watched by Govan and Kinsey (date unknown)

Coach Ray Shaw oversees a Birmingham City training session (date unknown). Top: Ready for training (date unknown)

Above: Geoff Vowden outjumps Blackburn defender Dick Mulvaney to head the first of his two goals past Sam Blacklaw at St Andrew's (circa mid 1960s). Below: The players leave by coach for an FA Cup fifth-round replay at Manchester United, February 1969. Facing camera left to right: Hockey, Greenhoff, Wylie, Murray, Vowden. In background, left to right: Summerill, Robinson and Vincent

Above: Training at St Andrew's days before the 1968 FA Cup semi-final against West Bromwich Albion. Left to right: Foster, Pickering, Bridges and Murray.

Left: Thomson (No 4) and goalscorer Vowden leap in the air (date unknown)

Above: An indirect free-kick causes mayhem inside the Stoke City penalty area. Left to right: Meilroy, Ritchie, Leslie, Kinnell, Auld, Foster and Thwaites (early 1960s). Below: 1970s crowd scene at St Andrew's, while opposite, top Blues fans outside Highbury, March 1968. Opposite page, bottom: Malcolm Beard completes his hat-trick in a 5-5 draw with Blackburn Rovers, April 1965

Above: Trevor Francis on the run at Manchester City, circa 1973.
Left: Bob Latchford in action, early 1970s. Below: Manager Willie Bell
(left) directs operation, September 1975. Opposite page: Trevor Francis
(centre) celebrates after helping Blues to the brink of promotion with
victory at Sheffield Wednesday, April 1972

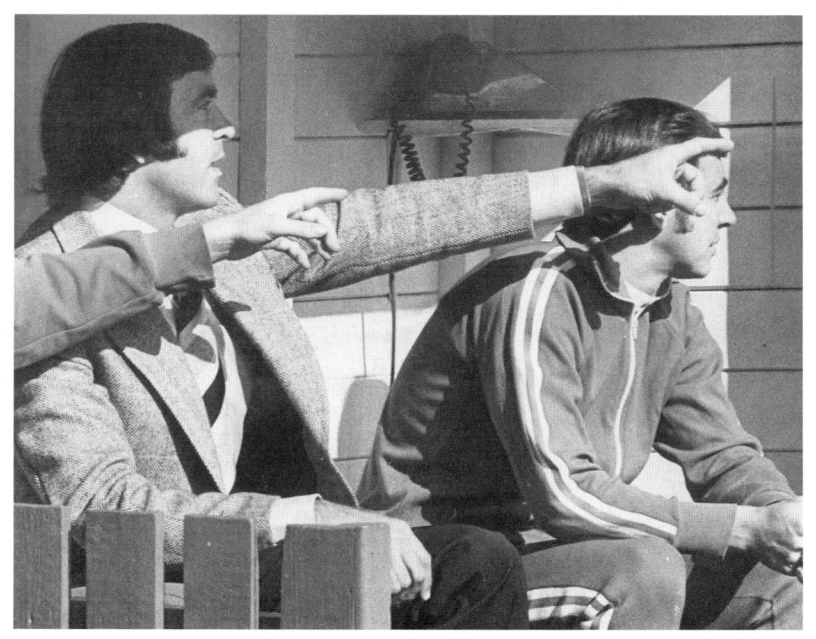

Above: Blues strike against Middlesbrough at St Andrew's (1970s).
Below: Trevor Francis challenges Liverpool's Ian Callaghan (mid 1970s)

At a time when City were struggling in the First Division, a newspaper story in March, 1979, featured fan Polly Mill. She believed she could do the manager's job and could be the first woman football boss in the top flight. Ahead of the game against rivals West Bromwich Albion, she said: "I reckon we've a good chance. They're a good team and have done well this season - but I hate them."

Keith Bertschin connects with an Alan Ainscow centre to give Birmingham City the lead against Sunderland at St Andrew's

**Above and left:
The Blue Revolution
fans' protest gathers
pace in the city, 1978**

Right: Fans make their feelings known. Below, middle: A walk-out demonstration at a match v Arsenal by fans seeking to depose the board of directors. Below, bottom: The protest within St Andrew's - although the original caption deemed the walk-out a flop, with only a small percentage of the 22,087 crowd leaving early with the match against the Gunners in progress (a 1-1 draw), March 1978

Above: Archie Gemmill shadows Kenny Dalglish during the 1-1 draw between City and Liverpool at St Andrew's, September 1980. **Opposite page, top:** The visit of Tampa Bay Rowdies brings the 'Wowdies' cheerleaders to St Andrew's (circa 1980). **Opposite page, bottom:** Jasper Carrott oversees the pre-match Evening Mail-sponsored Golden Goal competition (date unknown)

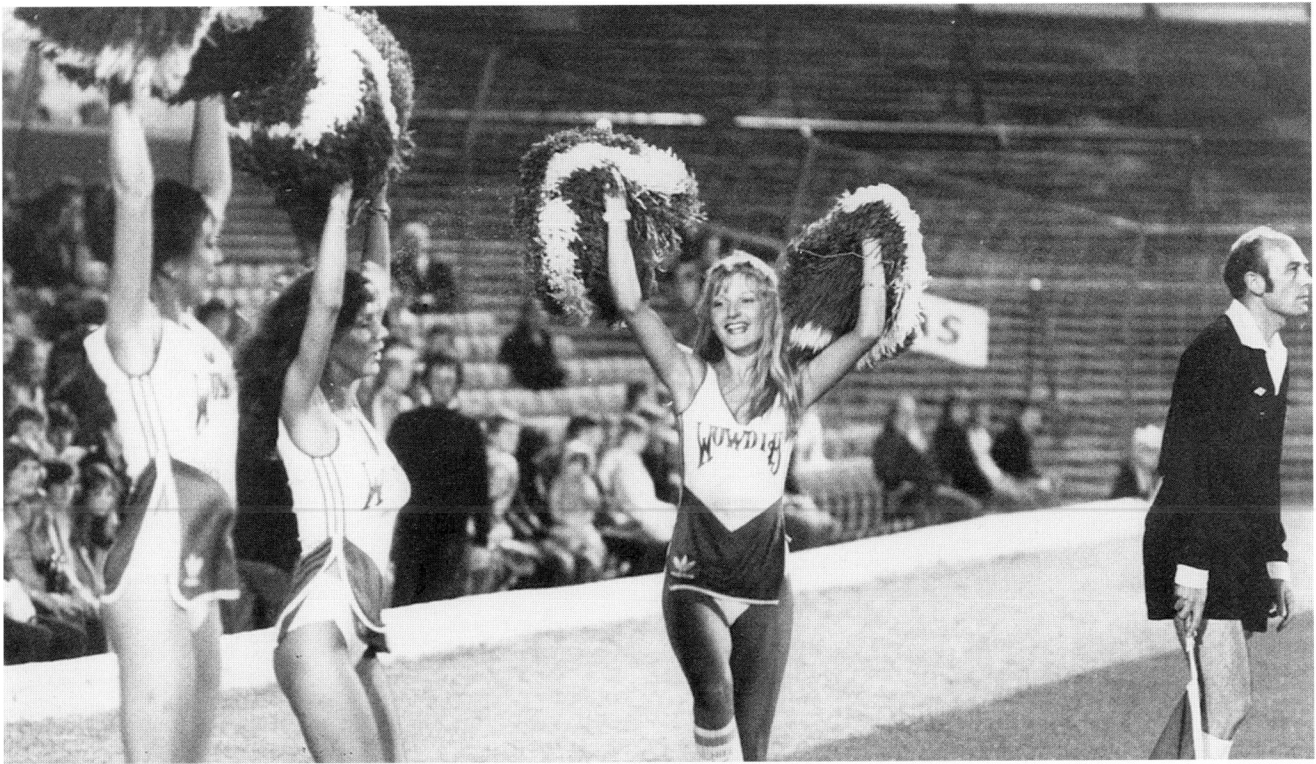

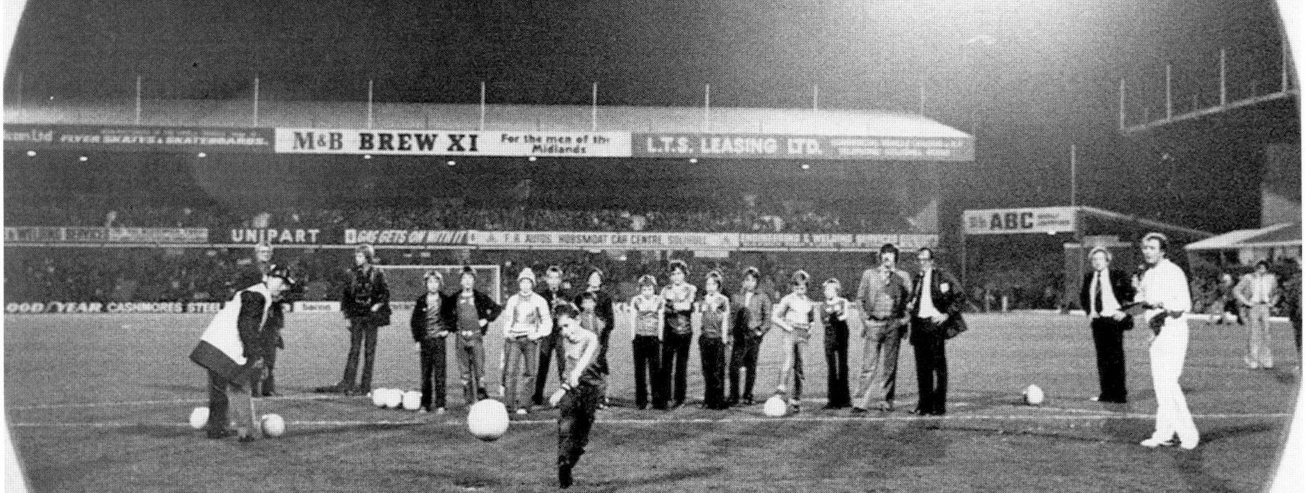
M&B BREW XI
For the men of the Midlands
L.T.S. LEASING LTD.
UNIPART
ABC

Above: Skipper Archie Gemmill taps home for Blues (circa 1980)
Below: Kevin Dillon sets Birmingham City on their way to a 2-0 win over Wrexham, February 1980

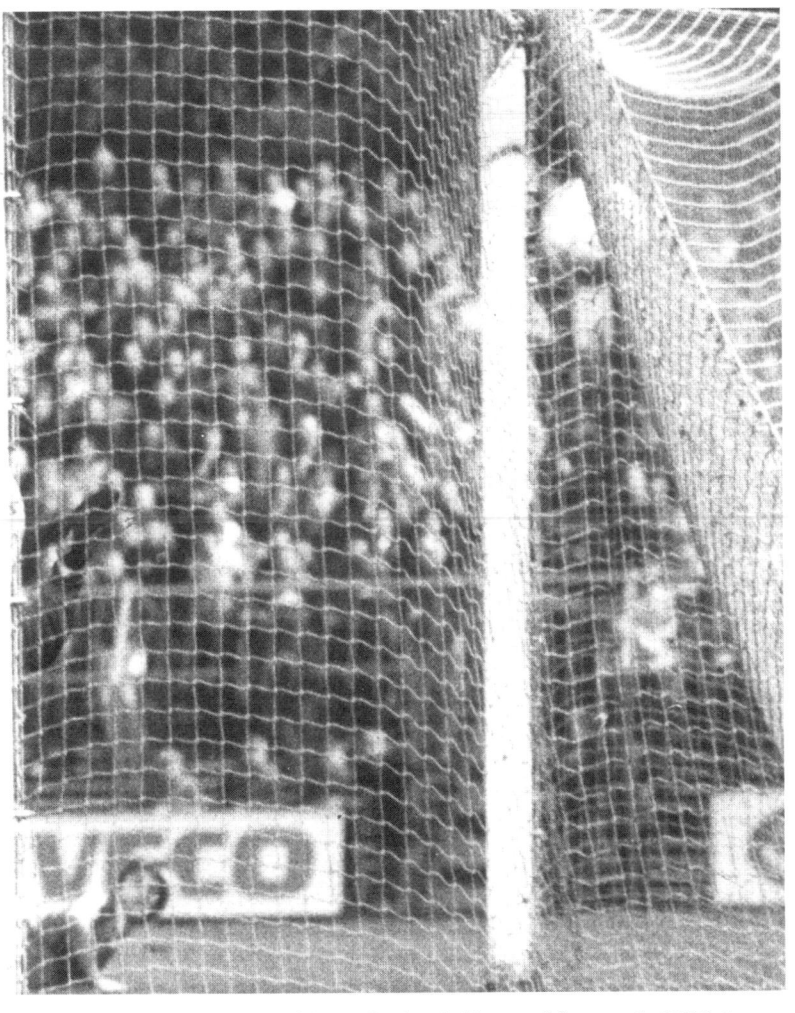

Above: The grounded Kevan Broadhurst watches his header find the target, with Mick Harford watching on (circa early 1980s).
Below: Robert Hopkins takes on Liverpool's Alan Hansen, early 1980s

Above: Blues players following their 1-0 win over Aston Villa in the Birmingham Senior Cup final in 1983.
Right: The little-known Atari Trophy is won, with Alan Curbishley holding the silverware.
Opposite page: Celebrations in the dressing room after clinching promotion to the First Division courtesy of a 2-0 victory over Cardiff City, May 1985 (top). Boss Ron Saunders, his grandson James and members of the squad on the balcony of the Birmingham Council House, May 1985 (below)

A parachutist flies into St Andrew's as part of pre-match entertainment, circa 1981

Above, left and below: Anti-hooligan fencing is introduced to St Andrew's, mid-1980s.
Above, right: Half-empty stands at Birmingham City, circa 1980s

Above: Blues players at the Balmoral Pub, Batley Green help raise money for the unemployed in the local Pool League by taking on the Balmoral Bullets and Balmoral Players (date unknown).
Right: Wayne Clarke heads home for Blues, circa 1984

Above: Blues coach Tony Brown shows his delight after hearing who Blues' opponents will be after the fifth-round draw, circa 1984. Below: Dave Mackay meets the Blues squad, 1989

Above: Action from a soggy St Andrew's, circa 1984. Right: Adrian Bird challenges Crystal Palace's Ian Wright, circa 1987

Des Bremner challenges Nottingham Forest's England star Neil Webb during an FA Cup fifth-round tie at St Andrew's, February 1988

Above: Tony Rees drives the ball goalwards against Reading, April 1987.
Left: Nigel Gleghorn celebrates a goal against Northampton Town, October 1989. Opposite page, top: Muhammad Ali is introduced to the St Andrew's crowd, May 1984. Opposite page, bottom: Trevor Francis and Bob Latchford show off their historic shirts which were being auctioned at a Blues reunion dinner, November 1990. The duo were flanked by former players from the 1970-75 era

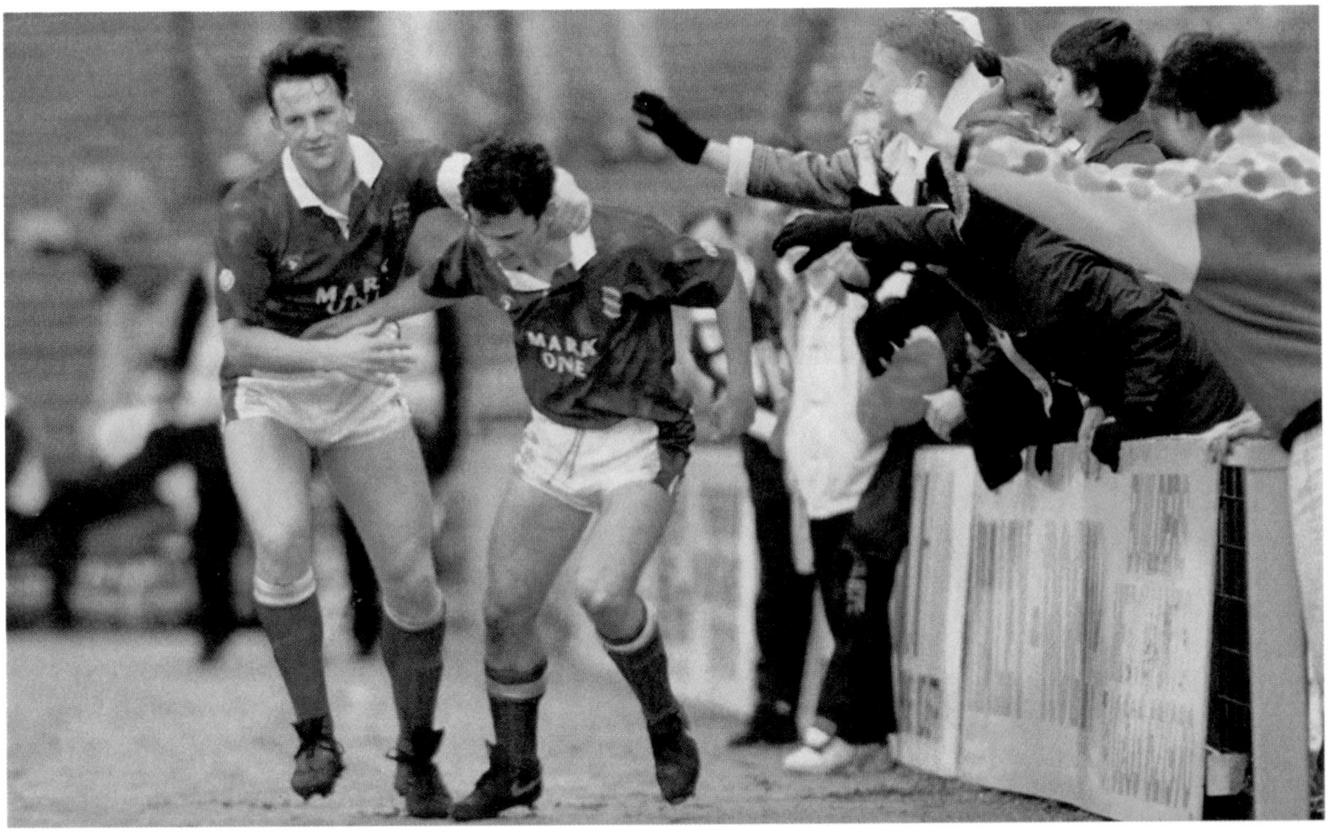
MARK ONE

BIRMINGHAM CITY
FOOTBALL CLUB
BIRMINGHAM CITY
LEYLAND DAF FINAL 1991
A568
YOV

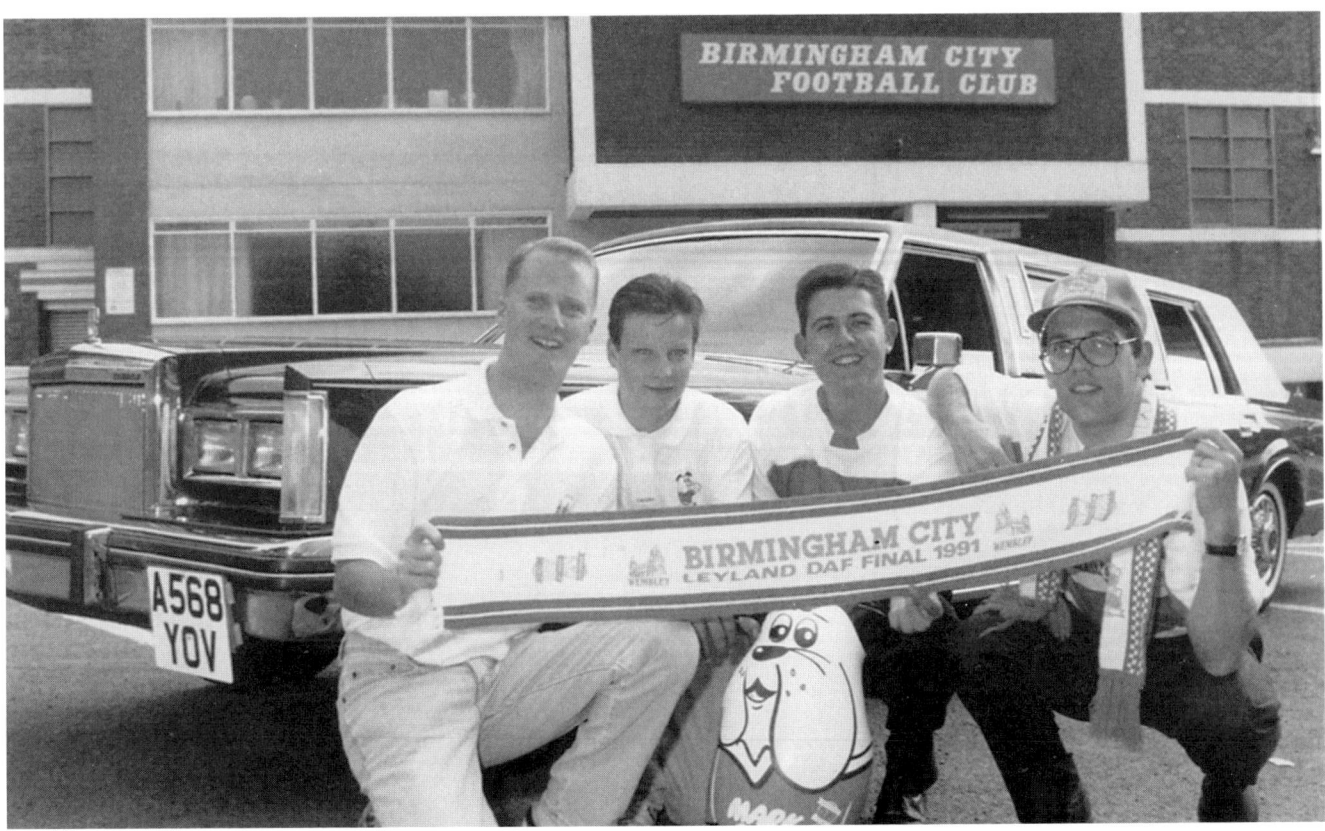

Above: Members of Sharmans FC who were set to travel to Cologne, and then planned to fly back to be at the 1991 Leyland DAF Cup final. **Left:** The Greenway family of Stirchley, Birmingham get ready for the final at Wembley.

Opposite page, top: Blues are on target against Chester City at St Andrew's, February 1991.

Opposite page, bottom: Fans Matthew Cole, Dean Lucas, Dean Wragg and Stephen Wragg preparing to travel to the 1991 final at Wembley in a hired Lincoln stretch limosine

Left: Manager Terry Cooper celebrates at the final whistle.
Bottom: Barry Fry takes the acclaim of Blues fans after guiding Blues to victory in the 1995 Auto Windscreens Shield final.
Opposite page: City supporters do their bit to back Blues at the 2002 First Division Play-Off final against Norwich City at Cardiff's Millennium Stadium

Above: Blues fans keep their eyes on the action, against Southampton in April, 2003.
Left: Geoff Horsfield celebrates his and City's third goal in the 3-0 victory over Aston Villa, September, 2002.
Opposite page, top: The modern St Andrew's.
Opposite page, bottom: Nicklas Bendtner scores what proves to be the winner against Hull City, September, 2006

INTO A NEW ERA

Natio
FOOTBAL
DIVISION 1 PLAY-
BIRMINGHA

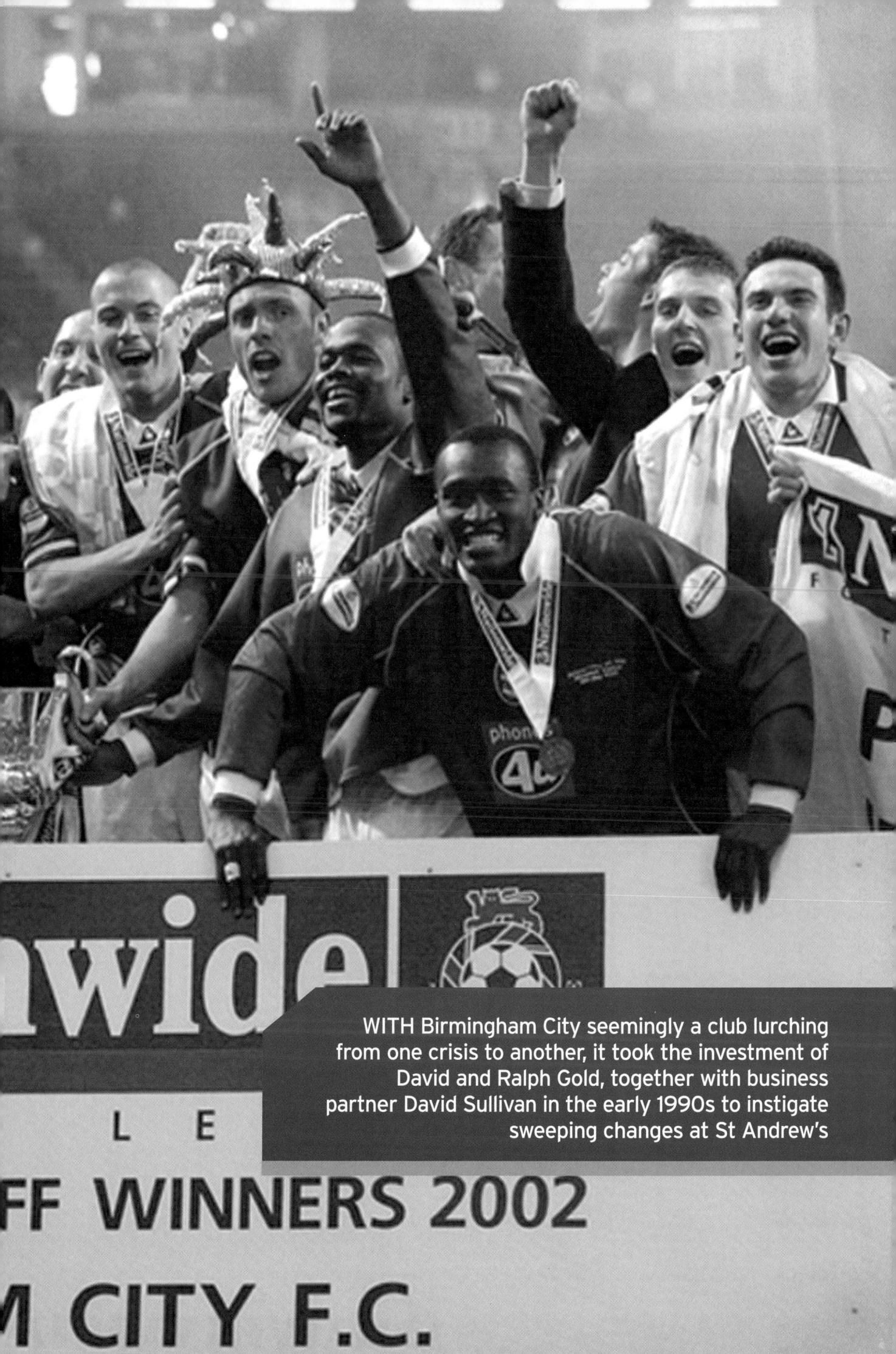

WITH Birmingham City seemingly a club lurching from one crisis to another, it took the investment of David and Ralph Gold, together with business partner David Sullivan in the early 1990s to instigate sweeping changes at St Andrew's

nwide

L E

FF WINNERS 2002

M CITY F.C.

When David Gold agreed to invest in Birmingham City Football Club, he wondered if he had made the right decision. It was March 1993 but there was not the hint of spring. "St Andrew's was in a dilapidated state," Gold recalls. "It was a shock. I had a picture in my mind of what I was expecting, but it was in such a state of disrepair that it was hard to comprehend. My first game was on a Tuesday evening, March 16, 1993, against Sunderland. Only two-thirds of the bulbs on the floodlights were working and the Football League had threatened action if we didn't do something to improve the lights. It was raining. It was a dour game. It was dark. It was dull. There were people standing in the rain looking extremely uncomfortable and unhappy. This First Division club was penniless and near to extinction. There were corrugated-iron fences around the ground and it looked as though it hadn't seen a lick of paint since Birmingham reached the FA Cup final in 1956."

As Birmingham celebrated a hundred years at St Andrew's, Gold was the chairman and the refurbishment of the ground was testimony to the vision of himself, his brother Ralph and to their business partner, David Sullivan. The Gold brothers had made their money from retailing and publishing, rising from poverty in the East End of London to a net worth of a billion pounds between them. They joined forces with Sullivan because they had mutual interests. Instead of competing with each other, they merged to bring the best out of each other. When they arrived at St Andrew's, they were bigger than Birmingham City Football Club. It took less than a decade to turn this club into a Premier League outfit, one that could compete with the likes of Liverpool, Arsenal, Manchester United and Chelsea. Birmingham had acquired legitimacy.

There is little doubt that 1993 is the most pivotal year in the club's recent history, for prior to that, for virtually the whole of the previous decade, Birmingham City was in dramatic decline. From the time Ron Saunders took over in February 1982, right through the reigns of John Bond, Garry Pendrey, Dave Mackay and Lou Macari, St Andrew's was not an edifying place in which to work. The club came to the brink of bankruptcy

Gary Childs in action against Middlesbrough in front of a sparce St Andrew's crowd, circa 1987

Birmingham City players enjoy their lap of honour following the 1991 Leyland DAF Cup success over Tranmere Rovers at Wembley

and the team found itself in the Third Division for three seasons from 1989. Attendances were down, morale was low on and off the terraces and hooliganism reared its ugly head.

On Saturday, May 11, 1985, when Birmingham should have been celebrating promotion back to the top flight, there was a riot at St Andrew's. Mr Justice Popplewell, whose committee looked into the causes of football hooliganism in the mid-Eighties, described events at St Andrew's as more like "the Battle of Agincourt than a football match". He was not exaggerating. The riot began when Martin Kuhl scored for Birmingham. "I scored and got flattened and then looked up and saw that they were all coming over the

fence," he says. "I thought, 'I best get out of here'. The irony was that I didn't score that many at Blues." Fighting broke out and riot police on horseback were called in to stop Leeds fans pulling down fencing. During the riot, a 12-foot wall collapsed and Ian Hambridge, aged 15, died. It was the worst day in the history of St Andrew's.

Despite finishing second in the Second Division, Birmingham's average home attendance in that 1984-85 campaign was a mere 12,522. In the top flight the season after, with Birmingham fighting to avoid relegation, the average home attendance was just 10,899. In 1986-87, with Birmingham just avoiding relegation to the Third Division, the average home attendance was 7,426. The nadir was

1988-89, when Birmingham finally did slip into the Third Division, which saw an average home attendance of just 6,289. A crowd of 4,686 saw Birmingham's final home match of the season, against Hull City. The second-largest club in the second-largest city had become virtually an irrelevance.

It seemed that the only way was up. Under Lou Macari in 1991, Birmingham won the Leyland DAF Trophy at Wembley against Tranmere Rovers. In the team that day were players, like Ian Clarkson, who clearly had the club's interests at heart. More than 40,000 Birmingham supporters were at Wembley. One might say that Birmingham's revival began that warm day in London. But Birmingham were still in the Third Division and still suffering financially. Under Terry Cooper, in 1992, Birmingham returned to the Second Division, but these were uncertain times.

During the period between David Gold agreeing to invest in the club and actually signing the contract, he witnessed at first hand the disillusionment that had swept St Andrew's. "In 14 league games during the pre-buyout period, the average crowd size was down to 10,000 per match, which was a fall of some 2,000 from the previous year," Gold says. "If that was the direction in which crowd numbers were going, it was going to be tough to keep the club in existence. Things had not improved hugely by the time of the buy-out in March 1993 but in the nine games between the buy-out and the end of the season, the average crowd jumped to almost 15,500 per game, enough to boost the season's average to 12,328."

The Gold brothers and David Sullivan acquired complete control of the club on May 8, 1993. Birmingham had just defeated Charlton Athletic 1-0 to avoid relegation back into the Third Division. There was a crowd of 22,234 at St Andrew's. All no doubt believed that the most significant aspect of the day was the victory. Not so. This was when Birmingham's fortunes improved dramatically. Life at St Andrew's was about to become a rollercoaster.

Terry Cooper left in 1993 and was replaced by Barry Fry, one of the most charismatic men in the game. He was just what Birmingham needed at that time. Just as significant was the appointment of Karren Brady, then 23,

Karren Brady, soon after being appointed the club's managing director in 1993

as a director. She was glamorous, she was intelligent, she was hard-working. Her arrival was seen as a gimmick but she quickly proved that she had the business acumen to help turn around the flagging fortunes of this once great football club. Crowds improved for the 1993-94 season but, interestingly, Birmingham were relegated back to the third tier of the English game (now known as League One). Whereas the

relegation to the Third Division in 1989 arrived like a dagger through the heart, the relegation in 1994 seemed a temporary measure. There was now too much style and substance about Birmingham. Everybody knew that Birmingham, as a club, was on the rise. And it was not going to let relegation get in the way of ambition, as Gold confirms. "Karren Brady had already shown that you could gain sponsorship if you were charismatic and successful, and bring the fans back through the turnstiles. Barry Fry we knew would excite the fans, punching the air and running up the touchline with his drive and passion. It was pure showbiz."

Birmingham returned to the First Division in 1995 and also won the Auto Windscreens Shield at Wembley. It had taken two years, but, at last, David Gold felt as though he was now accepted by the majority of Birmingham supporters. But Barry Fry's days were drawing to a close. The 1995-96 season did not provide a continuation of the progress made in the previous years.

Fry was adept in the Third Division but could not fashion a team good enough to gain promotion to the Premier League. Fry, a great motivator and a man who helped average players become good, had run his course at St Andrew's. He might have remained in charge had Trevor Francis not become available. But Francis was available and he replaced Fry during the summer of 1996.

Again, this was the right appointment at the right time. Season-ticket sales went through the roof. But Francis took his time to create a good team. It was only in 1998-99 that Birmingham looked capable of gaining promotion

Barry Fry - who helped the club back into the second tier, with Paul Williams and Steve Claridge

into the Premier League. Birmingham reached the play-off semi-finals, lost to Watford on penalties, and seemed to lack luck when it mattered most. Birmingham also lost in the play-off semi-finals to Barnsley in 2000 and Preston North End in 2001. This was a frustrating period that seemed to take its toll on Francis.

Birmingham's problem, as has been the case throughout their history, was their failure to overcome the final hurdle. Even when Birmingham lost on penalties to Liverpool in the final of the League Cup in 2001 they should probably have won. Birmingham always seemed to be unlucky. Trevor Francis the manager always seemed to be unlucky. But there were inherent problems, too, and Francis was no

longer fitting in. Gold could see it in Francis's eyes that Birmingham now needed a new manager. When Francis agreed to leave by mutual consent, he called a press conference. Gold was sitting at his side. "Who knows?" Francis said. "Some day I may return."

The highlight of the Francis era was the 4-1 victory against Ipswich Town in the League Cup semi-final, second leg at St Andrew's in 2001. This was a time when the players, supporters, directors and manager were in unison, celebrating a night that will go down in the club's history as one of the finest Birmingham City performances. Ipswich were in the Premier League, Birmingham were still in the First Division. And that was part of the problem. The Gold brothers and

Sullivan had created the environment for Premier League football. All it needed was a manager who could take the team that extra step.

Enter Steve Bruce in December 2001. Birmingham were in the middle of the First Division and, as a team, lacking direction. Bruce changed all that, led the team into the play-offs and a victory over two legs against Millwall. The final against Norwich City in Cardiff went to penalties and this time Birmingham were able to negotiate that final hurdle. For the first time since 1986, Birmingham were in the top flight of English football. The Gold-Gold-Sullivan-Brady bandwagon had occupied a parking spot in the most ▶

Diminishing crowds at St Andrew's failed to prevent new owners the Kumar Brothers show off their clothing range during half-time of a game v Bradford City in May, 1989

Karren Brady (right) was brought in by new owners David Sullivan and the Gold brothers, David and Ralph to help boost attendances at St Andrew's, which had fell to an average of 10,000 a game (above)

Penalty joy at last for Blues - a year after the League Cup final disappointment, Darren Carter's decisive spot-kick (top) sealed Birmingham City's return to the top flight in 2002 - after an absence of 16 years

Blues legend Trevor Francis (near right), who came so close to fulfilling the Premiership dream of co-owner David Sullivan (far right)

Steve Bruce is introduced by chairman David Gold to the media as Birmingham City's new manager, December 2001

exciting resort in the world. "Gaining promotion to the Premier League was one of the greatest moments of my life," believes Gold. "The excitement, the thrill of it all; going through the city in the open-top bus, the pageantry...it was an extraordinary experience. There were so many memorable experiences, especially seeing my mum in tears."

Of course, staying in the Premier League is more difficult than gaining promotion to the Premier League. In 2002-03, Birmingham might have endured relegation had it not been for the arrival of Christophe Dugarry on loan. Dugarry had won a World Cup winners' medal with France in 1998 and was believed to be at the end of his

career.

And yet, single-handedly, he scored the goals that enabled Birmingham to survive. They even finished above Aston Villa, which was something of an achievement given the contrasting fortunes of the two clubs over the previous two decades. Birmingham then spent serious money in trying to attract top-class players. Robbie Savage, Kenny Cunningham, Stephen Clemence and Clinton Morrison all arrived and the team looked capable of holding their own in the top flight, without ever suggesting that they could win trophies.

In 2004-05, Birmingham defeated Liverpool twice. The 2-0 victory

against Liverpool at home in February 2005 was, arguably, the finest performance by a Birmingham team at St Andrew's. Three months later, Liverpool defeated AC Milan on penalties in Istanbul to win the European Cup.

It was a defeat to Liverpool in March 2006 that highlighted the problems of the 2005-06 season. Too many injured players, not enough strength in depth and sheer bad luck. Birmingham were relegated on April 29, 2006 after they failed to defeat Newcastle United at home. The goalless draw turned St Andrew's into a funeral procession. When David Gold

Joy - Bruce is mobbed after guiding Birmingham to the Premiership in 2002

Andrew's were played to rows upon rows of empty seats and terracing, Wiseman was there. In the days when Birmingham were flirting with the obscurity of Fourth Division football, Wiseman was there.

The history of Birmingham City cannot be divorced from the life story of Jack Wiseman. He became a director in 1956 and was still the club's vice-chairman half a century later.

His enthusiasm for Birmingham City stems from his father, David, who, as an eight-year-old, used to gain free admission to Small Heath's matches at Muntz Street by offering to carry the players' bags into the dressing rooms. David 'Curly' Wiseman was born in 1885, the same year that Small Heath turned professional.

He became a director in 1928 and he became famous as the voice behind the FA Cup draw, in the days when the spectacle could only be heard on radio.

arrived in 1993, Birmingham were in the First Division. As Birmingham prepared to celebrate a hundred years at St Andrew's, they were back in the First Division (now the Coca-Cola Football League Championship). The difference, however, was that Birmingham and their stadium were now in good shape, whereas they had flirted with bankruptcy in the early Nineties.

For all the quality players that have represented the club over the years, there have been no more significant figures than the Gold brothers and David Sullivan.

David Gold credits Jack Wiseman with keeping Birmingham City together at a time when logic suggested that the club should have folded up. In the days when Birmingham matches at St

Despair - The Premiership adventure is ended, April 2006

David Gold (right) with Steve Bruce at Bolton, May 2006

David was thrilled when his son, Jack, joined the Birmingham board in 1956 - the year that the club reached the FA Cup final. Jack had developed his own special passion for Birmingham by regularly standing on the Spion Kop with his friends. But shortly after Jack joined the board, David, then in his early seventies, had to undergo major surgery to save his life. He lived on until 1978. When he died, he was 93, and his influence was felt way beyond St Andrew's. By this time, Jack was the vice-chairman.

The finest moment of his career with Birmingham came in March 1993 when

Karren Brady, acting on behalf of the Gold brothers and David Sullivan, who had just taken over the club, offered Jack the chance to remain at St Andrew's as a member of the board. This was effectively the past and the future merging into one. There is little doubt that the new owners had a feel for the club's history.

Brady says of that offer: "As a 23-year-old woman entering such a traditionally male-dominated environment, it was naturally a daunting prospect. But Jack's knowledge, persona and understanding of the mechanics of football were put fully at my disposal and gave me the

platform and confidence to help secure the future of this club and take it on to another level. Over the years, that support has never wavered and, throughout the difficult times that inevitably occur, Jack has been our rock."

Brady, born in April 1969, has already engraved her name into the history of the club. She was the first woman to hold a significant position with a leading English football club and she was responsible for Birmingham City's flotation in 1997, becoming the youngest managing director of a UK plc in the process. She has also been a non-executive director of Channel 4 television, has a seat on the board of Sport England, is chairman of Emap's Kerrang digital radio station and is a non-executive director of Mothercare.

She is married to Derby County footballer Paul Peschisolido. The couple have two children, daughter Sophia and son Paolo. On February 3, 2006, at the age of 36, she underwent brain surgery to remove an aneurysm. On February 5, she was transferred from the hospital's intensive care unit. The operation was a success and she was back in work long before the end of the season.

When Birmingham City endured relegation from the Premiership in Apriil 2006, Brady was in tears. She took it personally. The months of fighting for a new stadium, the weeks of rehabilitation from brain surgery, the intensity of wondering if Birmingham would survive...all of the emotions merged into one.

And yet it was a sign that she was, ultimately, a supporter like everybody else at St Andrew's on that April day. She felt their pain because she was one of them.

A few weeks later, when David Gold gave a lunch to launch his autobiography, Brady walked into the room to shake hands with those of us present. When she left the room, Gold turned to us and said: "This club is better because of Karren."

Indeed. History will treat her kindly because she quickly proved that she was more than a pretty face. Eventually, she became the public face of Birmingham's bid for a new stadium. She realised that football was moving on, that St Andrew's was limited, and that Birmingham needed to establish

Karren Brady watches training with Steve Bruce, July 2006

itself. The bid did not succeed, but she emerged with great credit. It is unlikely that she will give up. She is already thinking of how Birmingham can become a club of international stature.

She is, however, the fan with the ability to structure the immediate future of the club. In some ways, the same can be said of all Birmingham City supporters. The history of St Andrew's is really about them; the millions who,

over the years, have made the stadium what it has been and what it is today.

In times of hope and fear, they will sing that famous hymn, 'Keep Right On', and they will inspire the players.

Birmingham as a city owes its strength to its rich source of labour, its multiculturalism, and its personality. The same can be said of Birmingham City Football Club. St Andrew's is a reflection of what makes the city great.

It has been said that the finest goal seen at St Andrew's came from the right foot of Trevor Francis for Birmingham City against Carlisle United in the First Division in March 1975. Francis was near to the touchline, was more than 35 yards from the goal, yet somehow managed to score with an outrageous shot. 'It was the goal beyond the scope of most footballers,' beamed the report in the Birmingham Evening Mail. The newspaper was not exaggerating. The problem was, you needed to be at St Andrew's to witness it, for there was no blanket television coverage in those days. And yet, to those who were there, the noise that greeted the goal compensated for the lack of national attention. Football was not a reality television show. Spectator involvement was at its most intense.

Although they carried the name of the second-largest city in England, Birmingham City still had the look and feel of a provincial club. Francis would soon move and win the European Cup with Nottingham Forest. St Andrew's would soon fall into disrepair, until, two decades later, David Gold inspired a refurbishment programme that brought the stadium into its correct time space. But it took the arrival of such players as Christophe Dugarry, Emile Heskey and David Dunn at the start of the 21st century before Birmingham the club seemed as large as the city in which it played.

It is hard to know when, or even if, there was a golden era for St Andrew's. But great moments stand out. They always do. There are supporters still alive who remember when Birmingham scored their ninth goal against Liverpool in 1954. 'We want 10,' was the chant from the Kop at St Andrew's. And what of the night when First Division Birmingham defeated Premier League Ipswich Town 4-1 to reach the final of the League Cup in 2001. "Had I not been in the dugout as the manager, I would have been in the crowd cheering the lads on," was Trevor Francis's assessment of that extraordinary night. "I am always a Blue."

And to think, a century ago, the planned move to St Andrew's was met with little enthusiasm outside of the club. "We question whether the directors are wise in pitching their camp in such unsavoury surroundings," wrote the Birmingham Mail when the news emerged that the

Trevor Francis: "Had I not been in the dugout as the manager, I would have been in the crowd cheering the lads on".
Opposite page: David Dunn celebrates his goal against Ipswich Town, September 2006

club was acquiring the land.

When Birmingham announced, in 2004, that they were seeking to leave St Andrew's and build a stadium good enough to bid for the Commonwealth Games, the local newspapers were less conservative. They could see that St Andrew's had limitations and was not appropriate for a club with ambition.

The bid for a new stadium failed and, soon after, Birmingham endured relegation from the Premier League. When they began the 2006-07 campaign, nervousness encircled St Andrew's like a Mexican Wave. But as St Andrew's celebrated its 100th anniversary, it was looking better than at any time in its colourful life. "It is tense inside the stadium," Steve Bruce, the Birmingham manager, said. "But we need those supporters. They have been great to us over the years."

"St Andrew's is unique. St Andrew's is intense. St Andrew's is a magnet. There is no noisier ground than Birmingham's when the team are in the throes of yet another promotion battle." Those are the words of Simon Inglis, the football historian, in 1987. Inglis is a Villa supporter.

Joe Gallagher, the Scouser who played for Birmingham for virtually the whole of the Seventies, says that St Andrew's and the club are inextricably linked. It is hard to imagine one without the other. "When I played, the noise was often incredible," Gallagher says. "At some stadiums, you were concentrating so much that you did not notice the noise of the supporters, even when you played at the bigger grounds like Old Trafford. But at St Andrew's, no matter how much you were concentrating, you could always sense that atmosphere. I'm convinced we won some matches because of the crowd."

When Birmingham were at their best, during the mid-Fifties, St Andrew's was a large wall of noise. Gil Merrick was the goalkeeper in those days — one of the top five goalkeepers in the world — and he was in the perfect position to appreciate the real appeal of St Andrew's. "You didn't just hear the noise, you could feel it," he said.

There is a famous picture of Merrick during his time as the Birmingham manager. He is standing alone on the Kop at St Andrew's, looking wistfully into the distance. Behind him are the rows of terraces, the home to some of the most passionate supporters in the country. The terraces have gone, and Merrick stopped going to St Andrew's in 1964, but in some ways nothing has

The modern St Andrew's. Opposite page: Seats are installed, circa 1970 (top); the Kop, circa 1985 (bottom)

changed. St Andrew's is a modern stadium but there are still signs of the Merrick era. The Main Stand has barely changed since it was built, and the walk to St Andrew's looks similar to how it looked when Birmingham finished sixth in the First Division in 1956.

But how demographics have changed. When St Andrew's was built in 1906, it quickly became the preserve of the working-class male. That did not change for decades, even when the City of Birmingham quickly turned itself into a vast multicultural society. Males of mixed race started going to St Andrew's in large numbers in the Seventies, but it was the early Nineties before women enjoyed a significant

presence. Now, while a typical match at St Andrew's does not yet reflect the demographics of the city (and probably never will), it is no longer an occasion solely for the working-class male.

On the pitch in 2006, the average Birmingham player looks different to how he looked in 1906 and 1956. For most of the first 80 years of St Andrew's, Birmingham teams were usually made up of English, Scots, Welsh and Irish (with the odd Argentinian for good measure). When Birmingham played Hull City at home in September 2006, their team was made up of a Frenchman, two Tunisians, two Northern Irish, four Englishmen, a Swede and a Dane. Among the substitutes were an Australian and a Finn. The influx of

foreign players has given St Andrew's a more colourful feel.

In 2005-06, Birmingham paid their players more money than at any time in the club's history. Gone are the days when the players would go to the stadium on the same public transport as the supporters.

Nowadays, you can see Joe Gallagher sitting in the press box at St Andrew's, talking to the supporters with whom he works. He played at a time when there was a hint of glory but not a lot of money. After retiring, he still needed to earn a living. Those defenders who played for Birmingham a generation later — even those who lacked Gallagher's dominance in the air — earned enough in just a handful of seasons to last a lifetime. They stand

Martin Grainger (with Steve Bruce on the pitch) celebrates a goal against Sheffield United in April 2002

out a mile. They are often the ones who would never consider going to St Andrew's as a fan, once their playing days are over. Times have changed, the relationship between player and fan is diminished, but St Andrew's is still a theatre of dreams.

It was the backdrop to Martin Grainger's fine goal from 25 yards for Birmingham against Manchester United in 2004.

It was the backdrop to Emile Heskey's fine performance when Birmingham defeated Liverpool 2-0 in 2005. It was the backdrop to those European matches in the Fifties and Sixties when Birmingham led the way in the Inter-cities Fairs Cup. It was the backdrop to the momentous victory against Aston Villa in September 2002,

when Peter Enckleman scored the strangest, and most famous, own goal seen at the stadium. It was the backdrop to the pain of relegation from the Premier League in April 2006, when Birmingham drew 0-0 with Newcastle United and, temporarily, moved out of the limelight.

When St Andrew's was built in 1906, Birmingham were the ninth-best team in England.

When St Andrew's celebrated its 50th birthday in 1956, Birmingham were the 12th-best team in England. When St Andrew's celebrated its 100th birthday in 2006, Birmingham were out of the top flight and scrambling to return to what they consider to be their rightful

place.

It remains to be seen if St Andrew's will always be Birmingham's rightful place.

The limitations of the land on which the stadium stands means that progress will be difficult. Manchester United will turn Old Trafford into an 80,000-seat stadium, Arsenal have vacated Highbury and moved to a 60,000-seat stadium, Liverpool look set to have left Anfield by 2010 and moved to a 65,000-seat stadium.

No club can claim that a move away from their spiritual home is unacceptable, for economics must always intervene.

Sentimentality can only go so far in a game that is moving so quickly that not all clubs can keep up.

Birmingham are sure to move. The challenges of the game demand it.

But Birmingham City Football Club would never have been the same had a man called Harold Morris not chanced upon, in 1905, that "wilderness of stagnant water and muddy slopes".

His modern-day equivalent is Karren Brady, the club's managing director, whose vision of a new stadium was designed to move Birmingham City towards their next goal: that of international respectability.

Until then, St Andrew's will remain a unique home for a unique club with a unique following.

Above: Celebrations as Blues confirm promotion to the top flight, 1985.
Below: Birmingham City v Everton do battle circa 1950 - an era of relative success and stability for Blues